Date Due			
FEB 17 1977			

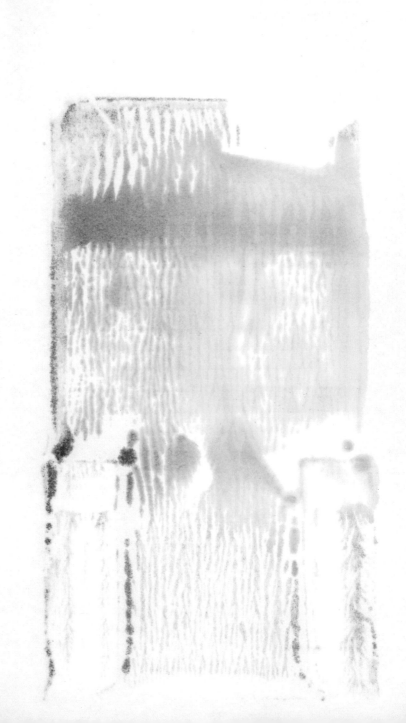

Tumbled House

IAN SCOTT

Tumbled House

THE CONGO AT INDEPENDENCE

London
OXFORD UNIVERSITY PRESS
NEW YORK TORONTO
1969

Oxford University Press, Ely House, London W.1

GLASGOW NEW YORK TORONTO MELBOURNE WELLINGTON
CAPE TOWN SALISBURY IBADAN NAIROBI LUSAKA ADDIS ABABA
BOMBAY CALCUTTA MADRAS KARACHI LAHORE DACCA
KUALA LUMPUR SINGAPORE HONG KONG TOKYO

Printed in Great Britain by
Hazell Watson & Viney Ltd, Aylesbury, Bucks

Keep the young generations in hail,
And bequeath them no tumbled house!

George Meredith,
The Empty Purse

List of Illustrations

Preface

'And you met Lumumba? Oh, how I envy you!' A Sudanese girl student gazed at us as she said this, so starry-eyed that we almost felt for the halo: it was as Christians in the early years must have looked at those who had known their Lord on earth. Our thoughts flashed back from the Embassy lawn in Khartoum where some university students were having tea with us: 'Yes, we lived next door to him and met him often.' But what could one tell this devotee about the realities of our eighteen months in the Congo, from the precarious high-hoped launching of the independent state to its disastrous capsize into chaos; and of the strangely febrile unbalanced person called Lumumba? What was the relation between the man and the myth?

The beginning, for us, was at the end of 1959. 'Let's not go' was the unanimous cry of my family when, one murky December evening, I brought the news to our London flat. They were sprawled in front of the television watching a particularly sensational episode of *Sanders of the River*—the Consul in the Congo was being slowly brought to the boil in a huge pot, surrounded by yelling tribes. 'We are going next month to Léopoldville,' I had announced. The awfulness of the prospect produced a moment's silence in which the rapid bumping of the plum pudding boiling in the kitchen next door added to the horrifying thoughts which were all too clearly crossing their minds.

We did not then imagine how very interesting and exciting our time in the Congo would prove to be; for the Congo was going to become a nine-months' wonder which would bring into the country at one moment 142 correspondents of the world's press and news agencies; when for months on end the crisis there would occupy much of the time of the United Nations in New York; when Lumumba's shooting star would trail its sudden brightness across the African sky. 'Bliss was it in that dawn to be alive,' quoted a young Nigerian friend to my wife on the Congo's day of Independence; and went on, 'At any rate if they do not feel that way, we do.' Nigeria's dawn too has been clouded since then; but in the Congo the high hopes and enthusiasm of the dawn were all too soon catastrophically darkened.

This book is not a history of the Congo crisis and does not pretend to be more than a modest contribution to the story and lessons of those days. It is concerned solely with the period January 1960 to the end of July 1961. Lest I be accused by some of bias, perhaps I should state at the beginning that I was biased—in favour of the Congolese and against all those who sought to impose what they wanted on the Congo, whether this was Belgium before and immediately after Independence, the U.N. and its agents, or the representatives of a variety of dictator régimes (black, white, and brown). Horrid things happened during the year and a half which we spent in the Congo; it was probably impossible for the Congo to be catapulted into independence in the 1960s without horrid things happening. These, however, would not have been so serious nor would they have lasted so long if the Congolese had got the disinterested and friendly help which they needed.

I

As Consul-General in the Congo, the only Belgian colony, I was to be nominally subordinate to the British Ambassador in Brussels, although for all practical purposes such as reporting and receiving instructions I dealt direct with the Foreign Office in London. Before leaving for Léopoldville, therefore, at the beginning of 1960, I paid a brief visit to Brussels to meet our Ambassador and Belgian government officials and some of the leading Belgian businessmen concerned with affairs in the Congo. Then, later in January, my wife and I travelled to Antwerp and sailed for the Congo in a comfortable Belgian ship bound for Matadi on the Congo river.

In my briefings in the Foreign Office I had been told that it was expected that the Belgian Congo would become independent in perhaps three years' time. This estimate was soon shown to be completely out of touch with the speed of developments. When my wife and I went to Antwerp on 28 January 1960 the newspapers announced that agreement had been reached the previous day, at the Round Table Conference in Brussels, for the Congo to become independent on 30 June of the same year. For most of the month of January this conference had been going on between the Belgian government and the Congolese political leaders—perhaps one should rather say 'Congolese would-be political leaders', as no effective political life had yet been allowed in the Congo. These Congolese leaders had indeed pressed—and this was a measure of their inexperience—that the date of Independence should be fixed even a month earlier, for May 1960; but they had accepted the Belgian contention that the extra month was necessary in order to devise satisfactory arrangements, particularly for an undefined 'transitional' period. It was not clear in the brief press notices which we read on the way to Antwerp whether such a period was to extend beyond 30 June; if so, what could possibly be the constitutional arrangements for it? Would not any such conceivable plan fall down on the sovereignty issue? How could Belgium retain powers in an independent Congo? Any such arrangements were bound to be repudiated as a derogation of sovereignty, once the country's leaders tasted full independence, for the same sort of reasons which had caused the failure of the British proposal for a joint

India–Pakistan Punjab boundary force, under the ultimate control of the British, to control migration across the Punjab border at the time of Partition in India in 1947.

The last days of the Belgian–Congolese Round Table Conference in Brussels saw unexplained manoeuvres, which gave the leadership of the Congolese delegates to Patrice Lumumba (brought straight from jail in the Congo at the insistent demand of the Congolese) instead of Joseph Kasavubu, the acknowledged father of the independence movement. On the last day, at the time when a decision in favour of a unitary Congo state had been agreed, Kasavubu vanished from Brussels and had to be replaced as leader of his own Bakongo tribal group at the conference. It was said that he had gone to Paris to discuss with French aluminium interests the setting up of an aluminium industry in the Bakongo region; alternatively, or in addition, that he had gone (perhaps in response to an offer of support) to discuss the chances of setting up a separate Bakongo state embracing those adjoining parts of the Lower Congo regions of the French and Belgian Congo and of Portuguese Angola where the Bakongo people lived. Here, as elsewhere in Africa, artificial territorial divisions created by the European colonial powers concerned had divided up an African people.

Kasavubu had already had one experience of Lumumba's strength in municipal elections in Léopoldville, where his own Bakongo party was strong (local elections being the only form of political activity which was then permitted). Perhaps Kasavubu saw the writing on the wall and decided that, as he could not hope to compete successfully with Lumumba for the leadership of a national party in a future parliamentary election covering the whole of the Congo (because he was too closely associated with the Bakongo people only), he should make a bid for his own separate Bakongo state.

He may have been encouraged in this hope by what seemed at the time (and since) an extraordinarily inept French intervention. According to the Belgian press at the end of January 1960, the French sent a Note to the Belgian government reminding them that, by an agreement of 1911, Belgium had given France the first option on any territory in the Congo which Belgium was giving up—an attempt to insure against British and German territorial expansion in Africa at that period. This agreement was irrelevant in the conditions of 1960 unless the French were toying with the idea of a united Bakongo state, possibly with its capital in the area constituted from part of French Congo. But such a claim on such grounds, with African nationalism rampant everywhere in the continent, seemed so futile as to be unbelievable for France officially to sponsor. And yet a leading Belgian banker, whom I had met the previous week in London, had assured me categorically that he knew the French to be behind a move to create a separate Lower Congo (or Bakongo) state. Perhaps Kasavubu was momentarily attracted—he could still be. The idea was not inconceivable if the Congo broke up; but this would only become practical politics if there were a general change in the climate of opinion. African leaders were then, as they still are, in no mood to redraw boundaries, however unjust and capricious they had formerly labelled them. And the handing over of territory under a treaty of half a century before, with lofty disregard of the wishes of the inhabitants, could certainly have provided no basis for any possible agreement.

However all that may be, the Belgian–Congolese conference in Brussels ended in agreement on a unitary Congo, with considerable devolution of power to the six provinces but with the international boundaries of the country remaining as they were. The mammoth task of drafting a new legal basis for the Congo's constitution began at once, as well as separate discussions on the financial implications of independence, particularly as regards the public debt of the Congo, some of which carried Belgian guarantees, and on the future of the many Belgian mining and other concessions. These represented vast investments in mining exploitation of copper, manganese, gold, diamonds, uranium, and so on, as well as rights over huge areas as yet undeveloped. Everything had to be rushed, and inevitably these intricate problems were not fully solved by 30 June. Indeed it was to take years of often acrimonious argument before agreements were finally reached.

The accepted time-table leading up to Independence was as follows:

1. 15 February 1960   Decision by the Belgian government on the recommendations of the Round Table Conference.
2. 18 February   Preparation of the necessary bills for the Belgian Parliament.
3. 8 March   Completion, printing, and introduction of these bills to Parliament.
4. 24 March   Vote on the bills by both Chambers of Parliament, after examination in committee and debate in public session.
Coming into force of the Acts.
5. 5–15 April   Preparation of lists of candidates for provincial elections in the Congo and for election to the Lower Chamber of the new Congolese Parliament.

6. 15 April–15 May   Period for electoral campaign in the Congo.
7. 16 May–6 June   Provincial elections and election for the Lower
                                      Chamber (Chamber of Deputies) in the Congo.
8. 15 June   Election for the Upper Chamber (Senate).
9. 20 June   Installation of the new Congolese government.
10. 30 June   Meeting of Congolese Parliament and
                                      Proclamation of Independence.

Towards the end of March, the dates for items 6, 7, and 8 of this programme were slightly advanced. Elections to Provincial Assemblies were to be complete by 25 May; and the election of senators by the Provincial Assemblies was fixed for 9 June. This left ten clear days for negotiations leading to the installation of a government by 20 June.

Our Embassy in Brussels reported to London the conclusions of the Round Table Conference with comments, of which I was given a copy on our departure by boat from Antwerp. I noted in my diary on 30 January:

I cannot think the Ambassador is right in saying that 'it is quite obvious that in the time available between now and the end of June, the Congolese cannot set up a fully-fledged administration. Accordingly, although the Fundamental Law [one of two laws which the Belgian Parliament would have to pass to implement the decisions reached at the Round Table Conference] will apparently say nothing about reserved powers, the Belgians will continue to exercise those powers which the Congolese are not ready to take over.' This seems more disingenuous on the part of the Belgians than their policy hitherto would indicate; and assumes a naiveté on the part of the Congolese which their recent achievements belie. It is much more likely to be a complete transference with, if the Belgians are lucky and skilful, agreements to keep Belgians in the administration for the time being, continue the concessions with minor modifications for the time being, and so on.

The next day completed the backcloth for our fortnight's journey to the Congo; my diary entry for 31 January records:

'The Round Table Conference discussed on Saturday the powers which Belgium would exercise during the transition period.' So said tonight's bulletin on the ship's notice-board. I read it after dinner with a couple of Belgian officials going back to the Congo after leave in Belgium. I said I wondered what 'transition period' meant—did it mean from now until 30 June or from after the elections in April and May until 30 June? One of the Belgians said that of course it meant the period *after* 30 June, during which Belgium would exercise powers over public order and so on. I said that might be twenty years, to which he replied that it should be. I appealed to another Belgian to say how he interpreted the phrase. He admitted that the Governor-General, in a speech three days before, had indicated a transition period after 30 June—there would have to be, as the Congolese were not ready to take over everything. If there was to be no transition after 30 June, why was he himself going back to the Congo with all the other officials on board? The first Belgian said, 'Do you think that on 30 June the Governor-General packs his bags and leaves and someone else, a Congolese above all, moves into his house?' I had not the heart then to say that that was what was likely to happen; and that the reason why they were all going back with no guidance about what was to happen was because events were moving too fast for them to have been told any more about the future of the Congo than they had read in the newspapers during the past week. So far I have met no official on board who seems to understand what has now been decided in Brussels—that 30 June 1960 for the Congo will be what 15 August 1947 was for India and Pakistan—the date of complete independent sovereignty—with no power residing in Brussels after it.

There was a cynical belief—realism, as they called it—on board, that Belgian policy was to scuttle out of the Congo politically in the hope of keeping as much as they could financially, economically, and commercially. The Belgians were prepared to move out as fast and as far politically as the *évolué* Congolese pushed them. The difficult question in the weeks ahead would be whether, as one returning official put it, Belgian business interests would consider the risks of such a policy too great. In that case, he said, the government in Brussels could be brought down as the Congo interests were very powerful there. But this development, he added, was perhaps unlikely.

The first use which we had heard of this phrase 'the *évolué* Congolese' had been by the Belgian doctor who gave us a clean bill of health in Antwerp—a requirement then for anyone going to the Congo for more than six months and met in our case by the most cursory examination. The doctor had served in the Congo and he talked about the forthcoming transfer of power; he mentioned the Dutch example in Indonesia as one not to be followed. And he ended his attentions to us with the remark that the Congolese were 'rather childish—all the *évolués* wear glasses as a sign of distinction'.

My wife and I were the only non-Belgians among the 170 or so passengers, all businessmen and officials returning with their families from leave in Belgium. They had large families too, some with three, four, and even five children, going happily back even though for some it would be to lonely and remote areas; some of their small children had been carried on board at Antwerp by smiling black stewards holding huge red umbrellas against the rain. The ship catered well for children, with a nursery and special mealtimes; it was clean, roomy, and comfortable, old-style British rather than the modern elegant Italian to which I and my wife had become accustomed in recent years while crossing the Mediterranean to the Middle East. The passengers, as we got to know some of them, were uniformly friendly, and gradually a sort of family party atmosphere developed, helped of course by the fact that a number of the Belgians already knew each other. A curious feature of the Belgian system of administration of their colony was that few of the returning officials knew where they were to be posted until just before the ship's arrival in the Congo; and some not even then. As the Congo included areas of widely differing climate and amenities, this was a worry for many of those with young families. One wife, indeed, told us that if her husband did not get sent to a town, she would have to return at once to Belgium with the children. None could foresee that in a few short months most of the passengers would be on their way back.

Endless discussion went on about how things would work out in the Congo. One Customs official who had served for fifteen years in the country thought that Belgian administration would continue after Independence under more or less nominal African control; that there would not in fact be much immediate change after the proclamation of Independence because the Congolese were not capable of running an independent state. He said however that he himself would be prepared to work under an African Minister in the true civil service spirit and be prepared to carry out orders even if he thought that they were wrong. He would advise against them in that case; but if ordered to carry them out he would do so although he would not thereafter be responsible for the consequences. Many of the older Belgian officials, he thought, would be prepared to do the same; but many of the younger ones would not. An agricultural chemist in the great research organization known as INEAC (Institut National pour l'Étude Agronomique du Congo) maintained that it was possible to teach the Congolese to do repetitive work, but sooner or later a day came when, for some unknown reason, they would fail to carry out some essential part in the routine and the whole thing would go wrong. He had a low opinion of their intelligence. I asked him if the Belgian administration had a good information service to explain to the Congolese what was happening. He did not understand what I meant at first and then said that the administration put out a daily bulletin 'but of course no one reads it'. The Congolese, he said, were incapable of understanding the meaning of independence. They could chant on occasion '*Indépendance, Indépendance, Indépendance*'; but as the various Congolese languages often dropped the first syllable, this became '*Dépendance, Dépendance, Dépendance*'. He added that Congolese students (learning in French) were very good at learning by heart without understanding; and stated that eight out of ten Congolese who were now at the two Congolese universities at Léopoldville and Élisabethville wanted to study law.

The ship's captain had an interestingly different point of view; his opinions were based almost entirely on his experiences at Matadi (the Congo's only port for the Atlantic Ocean). He said that after years of making calls there he was in favour of Congolese foremen of gangs to work on the ship rather than Belgian. No good Belgian foremen would ever go to the Congo, only navvies who had been failures in Belgium. One of them indeed had been a barber who needed to be taught his job by the Congolese.

There was a priest on board with whom also we had many talks. The Roman Catholic Church has played a great part in the development of the Congo and at the time of Independence there were some four thousand Belgian priests and nuns working all over the country, many in hospitals and leper settlements, and also in schools. Religious studies were the one branch of learning which the Congolese had for some years past been freely allowed to pursue, with the result that there were at that time about five hundred Congolese priests and several Congolese bishops. There was also an important Protestant missionary effort in the Congo, carried on chiefly by British Baptists and also by Americans and Canadians. These amounted to some 750 persons, including families, at the time of Independence. Our shipboard priest told us about the history of Christianity in the Lower Congo. Three and four centuries before there had been a flourishing Church in the region and there is an old cathedral of that time in the north of Angola. In the sixteenth century there had been a Lower Congo Christian envoy at the Vatican, who had died there and was buried in Rome; but then the Portuguese had started slave-trading which had, not unnaturally, put the Lower Congo off Christianity, and the Church went to pieces. There were some signs of revival now, but not very many. There was much talk of a cult called 'Kibangism', which was a mixture of Christianity and local tribal beliefs. In fact, as we learned later, this thirty-year-old movement owed something also to a premature bid for a share in political power. A relic of the former Christianity remained in the custom of some of the Lower Congo chiefs still to wear round their necks a cross, which had become a symbol of authority but had nothing any longer to do with the Christian religion.

T.H.—2

We asked the priest and an administration official one day what it would be like on board ship when the day came that there were Congolese passengers travelling. Would there be difficulties because of the easy and friendly social life which was part of the ship's routine? Both of them said that there would not be any problem because any Congolese who was sufficiently *évolué* to travel on such a ship would be accepted. They emphasized that there was no colour feeling against the Congolese, it was a social division. The Belgians were quite prepared to mix with people of any colour who had the same standards and way of life as themselves. In proof of this they said that any Congolese in Belgium would have no difficulty in finding accommodation—although of course there were very few of them at that time.

'Charity and patience—those are what you need if you live in the Congo—and patience mostly,' said the priest. He went on to say that the mentality of the Congolese was so different from the European that they did not reason in the same way nor were their reactions the same to any given set of circumstances. They could only grasp one thing at a time. This was in strong contrast with what the Vice-Rector of Lovanium University, himself a senior Belgian cleric, told us when we were being shown over the University a few weeks later. I asked him how the intelligence of Congolese students compared with that of Belgian young men who formed a large number of the university students. He replied that there was a very important difference: in all subjects where familiarity with the material objects of our civilization was a help— where for example children had played with toys and grown up in an atmosphere of practical, material things—the Belgians had the advantage. This had the result that Belgian students were much better at subjects like engineering. Where, on the other hand, pure reasoning was in question and it was a positive advantage to be untrammelled by any link with that kind of reality, as in pure physics or philosophy, the Congolese had the edge on the Belgians; and some of them were very good. I asked him if that meant that he thought the Einstein of the twenty-first century might be an African; he replied that this might indeed well be so.

Life on board continued its daily uneventful course. It was strange to read in the ship's library a book by Dr. Albert Schweitzer, written in the early years of the century when he first went to Lambarene, in which he describes the harmful effects of exposure to the sun and the particularly deadly danger of looking at the sun at the moment of its setting. He gave no real explanation of this curious belief, a product of the days before medicine knew anything about heatstroke and sunstroke; and as we watched the beautiful tropical sunsets from the ship we wondered what could have caused Dr. Schweitzer to adopt it. It was only when the war of 1939–45 came that all this seemed finally to change; then men began to work outside all day, stripped to the waist and with no head covering, in temperatures of 110 degrees and more.

Day by day, from the Canaries down to about latitude 7° South, we sailed through calm seas—it is never rough there, so the captain informed us. And every night the Southern Cross was a little higher in the sky while familiar constellations seemed to change their places.

Crossing the Equator was a different kind of experience. Those who had suffered previous initiation took care to see that newcomers to the southern hemisphere were suitably baptized. We were advised to appear in bathing costume for the occasion; and one by one went through an ordeal of having eggs broken on our heads, drinking lemonade out of chamber pots, and a whole series of even more revolting practices. My wife and I were let off comparatively lightly; but an unfortunate young Belgian police officer, who tried to get out of it and at the same time confessed to being afraid of what might happen to him, was taken last of all. He had watched the previous scenes of horror with ghoulish interest, and himself in turn received the worst treatment of all from a group of his colleagues.

Then one day the low coast of Africa appeared above the horizon and we turned east into the port of Lobito in Angola. Seventy-nine of the passengers disembarked—for those going to parts of the Congo the long railway journey to the south-eastern province of Katanga by the Benguela line through Angola was the quickest way of getting there. One Customs officer, due to take up his post on the Congo–Sudan border, was going to take his car by rail to Katanga and then drive north to his destination—a total journey of over 2,000 miles.

After a brief stop in Lobito, we headed north again until we were off the Congo river, a position easily discoverable both by the change in the colour of the sea and from the sudden depth revealed by the ship's echo-sounder. The volume of water in the Congo river is so vast that it scours a deep channel for many miles out to sea, far beyond the range at which the flat shoreland can be seen. We closed the shore and then took several hours to make our way up against the current to the port of Matadi, some sixty miles inland. It was fascinating to watch, hour by hour, the lush green country with rolling hills disappearing into the distance. We passed one sizeable town and a few straggling villages, but the impression was one of emptiness, a startling contrast with India, for example, where land such as we saw on the bank of the river would have been terraced and cultivated from the river's edge as far as the eye could see. That first impression of the Congo as an empty country (and Africa for the most part is an empty continent) was confirmed by later journeys. One could travel by air for literally hundreds of miles over the Congo and see only an occasional track and village. This must long continue to be one of the major limiting factors on development.

Our last two conversations on board, just before we went ashore at Matadi, reflected attitudes which we found to be general. A young police officer took an exceedingly gloomy view of the future and was much distressed at the sudden change of atmosphere in the countryside. Always before, he said, when you went through a village, people would wave and smile and bring their children to be seen. Now, he went on, 'You see pantomimes of throat-cutting and menacing gestures. It is the ingratitude of the blacks. Look at all we have done for them—why, there is not a city like Léopoldville in the whole of Africa.' And the young official who came on board to welcome us at Matadi, an anxious young man, perspiring heavily, was very worried—much more so than the Belgians on board, whom the problem had not yet really hit. This young official would be in the position on 30 June of becoming subordinate to the very people who had been working under him. He would not be willing, he said, to work under a Congolese Minister—it would be impossible.

Matadi was the end of the voyage and we parted from many of our fellow-passengers who were travelling onward by the cars which they had brought with them. The others, like us, went by train from Matadi to Léopoldville. Between the seaport and Léopoldville, 250 miles further up the river and 1,250 feet above sea level, the Congo river flows in a succession of fearsome rapids which make navigation impossible. This was one main reason for the long isolation of the Congo; the country lay cut off behind these rapids until the building of the railway, whose construction in the 1890s is said to have cost the lives of one Belgian engineer and ten labourers for every mile of the track from Matadi to Léopoldville. Chinese labourers were brought in, amongst others, to build it; one of them, it was sometimes said, was a grandparent of Kasavubu. It is hard to realize that until Stanley made his way down the river less than a hundred years ago from the other side of Africa—not knowing at the start of his journey if the river he was following would turn out to be the Congo or the Nile—all the huge territory of the

Congo was as unknown, almost, as another planet is today. The unnavigable stretch of river, which we now avoided by the rail journey, lies for some miles almost parallel to an ancient, now dry, channel. It would, according to detailed studies made in earlier years, be easy and relatively cheap to divert water down this old course and generate as much electrical power as would equal one-fifth of all the electricity consumed in the U.S.A. But what would this energy be used for? There was neither the population in the region to be employed in an industrial complex of any size, nor the population in the whole of the Congo and in neighbouring countries, nor even in all of Africa, to absorb the products of such development. Maybe in a hundred years' time the world will be sending its alumina to be processed there and the banks of the Lower Congo river will be the African Ruhr; but its full development is not likely this century.

We had done our best during the fortnight's journey to extract from our Belgian friends information about the conditions and the people in the country in which we were going to live; but it was neither a clear nor a happy picture which began to take shape. Many Belgians, if one could sum up these various impressions, seemed to like the Congolese as a sort of sub-human species. None, so far as we could find out, had any Congolese friends or had ever entertained Congolese in their homes. Few felt that they knew them well enough or trusted them sufficiently to work with or under them. This became more evident in the immediately following weeks and months.

2

So we came to Léopoldville, and to the Consul-General's house which was to be our home—a largish, clumsily built house on the banks of the river, looking across to Brazzaville, capital of the ex-French colony of the Congo, and up-river to Stanley Pool, the wide lakelike expanse where the Congo flows slowly before narrowing for the rapids below Léopoldville. Brazzaville was on the opposite bank across about two miles of water, with low hills behind. On our side there were only a road and a grass verge with flowering trees between our house and the steep bank of the river—a road lined with pleasant houses set in large gardens full of bougainvillaea, hibiscus, frangipani, and the spectacular 'flame of the forest'. Eastwards this road led in to the city; westwards we were next but one to the house where the Governor-General lived, which later Lumumba occupied during his brief time as Prime Minister. A few hundred yards further on, the road opened out on to an imposing vista such as all planned cities incorporate: it led from the High Court at one end to the new Residence which was being built for the Governor-General, overlooking the river. The latter was rapidly to be adapted to become the new Parliament Building; but still incongruously in front of it the statue of Léopold II on his great bronze horse faced the long vista—he was the Belgian King who had acquired by 1884 the vast territory of the future colony.

The Belgian Congo, the second largest country in Africa, with nearly a million square miles and 14,000,000 inhabitants, lay in the very middle of the continent, and the map of it (opposite) looks something like a broad ivy leaf—the narrow stalk westwards to the sea, the far tip slightly drooping towards the east and south. The river and its tributaries are the veins; the Congo river itself, the central vein, makes a great sweep to the north across the Equator and then turns west and south again, all its middle course being through the huge belt of equatorial forest bordered north and south by savannah lands. The eastern edge of the leaf is curled up in the north into the Mountains of the Moon. South of them lies the 450-mile-long Lake Tanganyika and then comes the south-east corner where Katanga points down into Rhodesia. Here in the east and south-east lies the mineral wealth of the country—

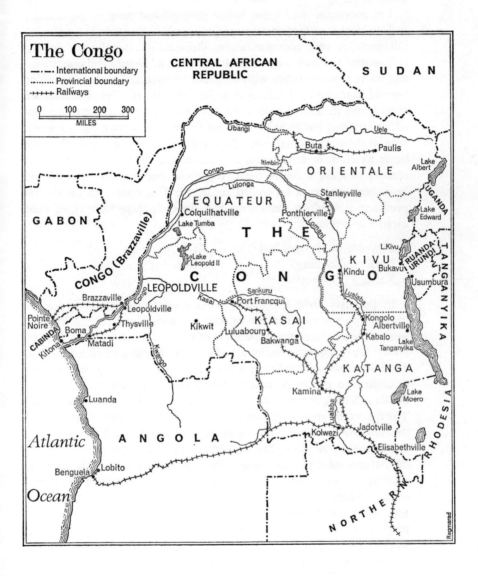

diamonds, tin, copper, cobalt, manganese, uranium, and no doubt other minerals yet to be discovered.

The enormous river basin is the geographical basis of the country and the river is all that unites it geographically. Everything else divides. Distances are vast, communications difficult, and populations isolated and scattered. There are also great contrasts of climate and conditions, and many separate tribes with different languages. There was nothing but the river and the Belgians to make a nation. The Belgians achieved control over the many tribes and united the country under a competent administration; but they built up no national consciousness. Léopold-ville, at the edge, so to speak, of the stalk of the ivy leaf, though at the lower terminus of river transport, was too far from most parts of the country to make a centre for any purpose but administration. From here, however, were controlled under the Governor-General the six provinces into which the Congo was divided; these were (with their capitals in brackets):

Léopoldville (Léopoldville)	Kivu (Bukavu)
Kasai (Luluabourg)	Orientale (Stanleyville)
Katanga (Élisabethville)	Équateur (Coquilhatville)

In February 1960 Léopoldville, the capital of the colony, was an impressive city to find in the middle of Africa. Some 20,000 Belgians lived there in a total city population of perhaps 400,000. They were by far the largest foreign community, but there were also small numbers of other foreigners, including about 250 British. The city had a river frontage of a couple of miles, and included fine streets and double boulevards with, in the centre, blocks of seven- and ten-storey buildings. The residential areas stretched for miles round about and sometimes up the hills near by. There was, however, complete housing segregation of Europeans and Africans. Servants left at dusk and rode their bicycles to the African suburbs, anything from two to ten miles away. Some of these in turn were admirable housing estates, with electricity and water-borne sewage; others were part slum, part old village, but these latter were scheduled for transformation as part of a development plan in progress. If an evening party was being given in the European sector, servants would stay, but they required a pass to let them through the police cordon on returning late at night to their houses. There was no legal sanction behind this kind of apartheid, and a few Africans could frequently be seen in the pavement cafés in the daytime drinking beer with the mainly Belgian clientele. There was also the economic fact that no African could afford the kind of house the Belgians lived in: the richest Africans were the junior government employees.

At the beginning of 1960 there were some 10,000 Belgians in the top four grades of the administration, and 10,000 Congolese in the bottom four grades. The requirements for entry were such that, when taken in conjunction with the educational opportunities open to the Congolese, it was virtually impossible for any Congolese to get into the senior grades. A university had been founded only in the early 1950s named Lovanium (a daughter foundation of the University of Louvain in Belgium); it was beautifully located on a ridge of hills about ten miles from Léopoldville and some 2,000 feet above sea level. The buildings were very fine with an ultra-modern chapel and splendid lecture rooms and students' quarters—the latter as good as in any modern British university I have seen. The Rector was a senior Belgian cleric who was also a nuclear physicist, and the University possessed the only nuclear reactor then in Africa. But no Congolese students could enrol for law studies until 1958; the Belgian professor of law told me that he was not allowed to accept Congolese as a matter of policy because the study of law was dangerous—it created future politicians. In 1960 two-thirds of the students at the University (which numbered only a few hundred at that time) were African young men; and there were about thirty-five Belgian, but no African girls. Measures were in hand to build up the second university at Élisabethville in Katanga, but that institution was in 1959–60 altogether smaller and more limited in scope than Lovanium. The same story repeated itself in the schools. The largest secondary school in Léopoldville had 1,600 pupils, but only a handful were Congolese.

Technical education was, however, another matter. This was done well and to very high standards; and the Union Minière, the copper-mining company in Katanga province, maintained its own, first-class technical schools. I saw during 1960, in a modern electrolytic smelter in Katanga, the most highly-skilled job of remote control of the movement of liquid copper from the furnaces into moulds being done by an African, whose grandfather had probably never seen a wheel. Drivers and fire-men of trains were Congolese. I never travelled by train in Northern Rhodesia, but I understood that when a train crossed from the Congo into Northern Rhodesia, out stepped the black driver and in came a white; as well as white waiters to replace the Congolese restaurant-car attendants. Similarly with river traffic, a most important means of com-munication. The service, for example, to Stanleyville, capital of

Orientale province, 1,100 miles up-river from Léopoldville, included four-decker passenger-carrying ships, to which might be lashed barges of up to three and four thousand tons. The Congo river runs fast, and the navigation required, to get not only to Stanleyville but up some of the tributaries, was of a high order. An increasing menace to navigation was the steady spread of water hyacinth, a virulent weed which proliferates luxuriantly and can completely clog even quite a large river. The means of fighting it—e.g., spraying by launch far up the tributaries—were not such as could easily be developed in the hectic days and months before and after Independence. But in our first months in the Congo the river steamers continued to ply regularly to Stanleyville, and also provided the only reliable communications up two of the main tributaries of the Congo. Where river steamers could not travel—because of rapids—trains took over before the steamers resumed (as after the stretch of rapids for 100 miles above Stanleyville). From Port Francqui on the tributary running from Kasai province the railway link continued the line to Katanga; and this route, in spite of three transshipments—at Port Francqui, in Léopoldville, and at the seaport of Matadi—was a main outlet for the Katanga and Kasai minerals. The whole of this vast system of integrated movement by rail, river, and port was organized by OTRACO, the 'parastatal', as it was called, communications undertaking.

A ferry steamer, every hour or so, crossed regularly during the day from Léopoldville to Brazzaville; it was always a colourful spectacle with gaily-dressed Congolese women going across for marketing. Public transport within Léopoldville was by bus—frequent, reliable, and reasonably cheap—and by taxi. These two cities facing each other across the Congo river symbolized in a way the two kinds of European influence which adjoining European countries had brought to the middle of Africa. Léopoldville was rich, disciplined, clean, spaciously laid out, and spreading for miles around; Brazzaville was in comparison small, untidy, rather scruffy, like a French provincial town, more human however than its neighbour across the water and looking as if it might even be gay on occasion.

It was important to get to know as many senior officials and Congolese leaders as possible, and our entertainment was directed to this end. On a number of occasions senior Belgian residents in Léopoldville met in our house Congolese politicians to whom they had never spoken before; and in one surprising instance the wife of the Provincial Governor proved never to have even heard the name of someone she thus met with us who was clearly destined to become at once a leading Minister in the independent Congo. It was not so much that the Belgians consciously avoided any contact with the Congolese; it was simply that it had never entered their minds that this might be a good thing to do. The reverse side of their 'realism' was a complete lack of imagination, and this conditioned their behaviour even after it had become clear that the Congo was on the way to early and full independence. In 1959 Western consulates in Léopoldville had been warned by the Belgian colonial authorities not to get on close terms with the Congolese. This ban had been relaxed by the time of our arrival, and a fortunate chance soon afterwards enabled us to show at once where we stood on this. It happened that a Tanganyika Minister had to remain for a few days in Léopoldville waiting for an air connection (routes ran north and south in Africa and it could at that period be a tedious journey to go from, say, Tanganyika to Lagos). We invited him to stay with us and found him a friendly and charming guest. It was thus possible to use his presence to invite senior Belgian officials to meet at dinner not just any African, which they might have refused, but a Minister of the Crown. The experience was obviously new; and the first morning provided a laughable object-lesson. Our houseboy had spent the night, as was the custom for his kind, miles away with his family; he knew that a guest had arrived the night before but he did not know that he was an African. When he brought the breakfast to the three of us at the table, therefore, he stood stock-still, eyes popping out of his head at the sight of a black man sitting with my wife and me.

On 20 February I paid my first call on the Governor-General. He told me that he thought the worst was now over; it would have been very bad if the Round Table Conference in Brussels had broken down, or if the African delegates had split and quarrelled among themselves, or if no decisions had been reached. Now that they had agreed on an interim advisory council of six members, he thought that arrangements would work out all right. Whether or not the Governor-General was expressing an optimism he did not really feel, this was to take a very limited view of 'the worst'. The remarks of many people whom we met in those early weeks showed that, since a riot of 4 January 1959 in Léopoldville, morale had been steadily deteriorating; and Europeans had not felt at all easy when going outside the town, unless in a group. It was from that date too that the change in the feelings of many ordinary Congolese to the Belgians had begun, of which the young

Belgian police officer had spoken to us at Matadi. It was therefore in convoy that the Belgians who had been on our ship and had brought their cars with them drove up from Matadi to Léopoldville; and the papers had frequent tales of road-blocks at night, or of traffic signs thrown across, on the Léopoldville–Matadi road. The common African practice of attacking the occupants of a car which has injured an inhabitant of a village acquired an additional edge to it; a nasty incident occurred when a missionary couple following unwittingly behind a car which had been involved in an accident (but had driven on) were stopped and very seriously beaten. Even from the European-occupied suburbs of Léopoldville itself people were advised to take particular routes and avoid lonely stretches of road by night, and not to go into the African part of the city except in company with others.

The riot of 4 January 1959 had resulted from a clash between a football crowd and a political meeting which was breaking up when the crowd was dispersing. Many people had been killed and there had been a certain amount of rioting as disorder spread, with looting and thuggery by gangs of unemployed youths. This occurred on a Saturday afternoon and though serious was not in itself a particularly catastrophic incident, nor should it have deflected Belgian policy as it did. It was however the first in which deaths had occurred, and it exhibited the Belgian system of colonial administration at its most ineffective. The Governor-General had had to refer to Brussels for approval of the use of force, which he considered necessary, and, so it was said, the Belgian Minister concerned had been away shooting for the week-end without leaving his telephone number. Twenty-four valuable hours had therefore passed in uncertainty, and the final result was very much more far-reaching and upsetting than it would have been if prompt local action had been possible and had been taken.

A dinner at the Governor-General's house on 10 March, early as it came after the Brussels conference, was in its way for us the epitome of the end of one era and the beginning of another. It was a formal occasion with some sixty to dinner; very hot and sticky with no ventilation or fans in the dining room and a long-drawn-out meal. When at last we left the table there was nowhere to sit. We stood around on swollen feet until the senior guest (the American Consul-General) mercifully took his leave and released us. Four Africans had been invited, mayors of the African communes—or local administrative divisions—of Léopoldville The first three who arrived made excuses for the absence of their wives, who were each apparently expecting a

baby, and the table plan was three times quickly amended. The fourth
arrived with his wife and baby. The Governor-General's lady, receiving
at the door, threw up her hands in horror and told the A.D.C. to remove
the baby; he successfully did so and had it sent home. The mother
spent a very dull evening—as it happened, next to me—unable, for lack
of knowledge of any language but her own, to exchange a word with
anyone at the table and eating unaccustomed food in unaccustomed
ways. One other Congolese came who had been invited not for that
night but for an occasion some weeks earlier. With the greatest difficulty he was induced to take a seat which had a place-card for someone
else; but he was not happy until a whole lot of place-cards had been
shuffled round, with mounting irritation among those affected. Clearly,
this formula for a gubernatorial dinner was out for the future. It had
been '*dépassé par les événements*'—a phrase which became all too
familiar and accurate a description of many a subsequent plan.

While I paid my official calls, my wife paid hers. The wife of the
Commander-in-Chief, General Janssens, a competent and hard Belgian
officer, said (perhaps reflecting her husband's views) that she felt things
had gone altogether too quickly. The Congolese needed the Belgians for
at least another twenty years; and she felt that the ordinary Congolese
people were bound to suffer by the rush of change. The Provincial
Governor's wife, living in a splendid house with a garden looking over
the rapids of the Congo river below Léopoldville, was very sad and de-
pressed. She and her husband had spent thirty years in the Congo. She
had no understanding of or sympathy for the changes already taking
place and the greater ones impending. 'It was always so nice here, no
trouble; we used to visit each other and talk of dresses and new curtains—
now it is politics all the time and who knows what is going to happen?'
Some there were, however, both husband and wife, who were greatly
interested in the changes and ready to talk about the way things might
go. Sometimes we could have an evening group including some of those
Belgians and young Congolese leaders; but that did not often work.

On one occasion we had a senior Belgian official and his wife to
dinner, together with Lumumba and one or two other guests. Joseph
Ileo (who in 1961 became Prime Minister) and his wife came in late.
Lumumba launched into a tirade about imperial oppression and how the
Congolese had been downtrodden, in rude and forthright language.
This produced an interesting if sticky dinner party, but our Belgian
guests took it very well. One could see then Lumumba's power over
crowds; he spoke well and could offer a heady brew of revolutionary

talk. When the Ileos arrived, Lumumba completely changed his tune. Ileo was a very different kind of person and a much more thoughtful and stable character. He began explaining about a political institute which he was starting, a subject with which Lumumba was out of sympathy; he was clearly rather taken aback both by the arrival of Ileo and the turn in the conversation. Mme Ileo was a very unsophisticated person, expecting her seventh child. She spoke a little French, however, and got on well enough, though evidently without very much understanding of things—after dinner, for example, she asked my wife, pointing to me, 'Is he your husband?', and gave a great sigh of relief when an affirmative answer was given. We asked Lumumba why he preached hatred of the Belgians. He replied that we ought to be glad that he did so at that time, because 'If we talk like this we are much less likely actually to have violence. You have no idea what we have to put up with and how it rankles in us, and we have to work it out of ourselves like this.' Altogether that was not an easy evening. Our houseboys were clearly intrigued by Mme Ileo, no doubt the first Congolese lady they had ever seen sitting in that house. They hung around in the dining-room doorway to watch her.

On another evening we had Philippe Kanza to dinner along with one or two others. Already then it was becoming obvious that the Kanza family were not going to co-operate with the new Congolese political leaders. The Kanzas were a remarkable group, the old father, Daniel, claiming indeed to have been, with Kasavubu, one of the founders of the movement for independence and to have been replaced by Kasavubu as leader of the Bakongo tribe. Daniel Kanza was a staunch Protestant who had served thirteen years in the army, but had brought up his four sons as Roman Catholics as that was the only way in which they had a hope of getting a higher education. All were clever and made the most of their opportunities. The family had been helped by Unilever to set up a printing establishment in Léopoldville—the father said that he had been offered the printing machines free by the Czechs but had refused them as they did not wish to be beholden to the Czechs for favours. A Belgian bank had declined to make the necessary loan. On the occasion of the evening in our house Philippe Kanza refused to accept advice, from a fellow Congolese as well as ourselves, that the family should make their peace with Kasavubu over the leadership question. He said that even if his brother Thomas (later Congolese Ambassador in London) could be persuaded to make his peace, he, Philippe, would 'unpersuade him again—I cannot accept that they should insult my father as they have done.' His fellow Congolese guest said, 'You mustn't think of personal things, you must think of the Congo,' to which Philippe Kanza replied, 'What Congo are you talking about?'

General Janssens and his family came to a meal with us one day and gave a potted history of the Congo. The Belgians had never wanted a colony, he said. 'None of that sort of trouble for us—we will stay safe at home,' had been their thought. It was all King Léopold and then a small number of educated men who followed the King; they built up the structure of the Congo. The Belgian State refused more than once to have anything to do with it. Then the last time King Léopold offered the Congo to the State (in 1907), the colony had just begun to pay and the Belgians said, 'Well, come, perhaps there is something in this colony business after all.' The structure that had been built up over half a century was very efficient, but its balance was very delicate because the administration was so thin on the ground. 'Now along come those peasants in Belgium with their *sabots*,' went on General Janssens, 'and give a few hearty kicks. "What, you haven't progressed past this? *Tiens!* You haven't educated these people. *Oh là là!*"—and the whole fabric collapses. Then the people in Belgium say, "We always knew that a colony meant trouble—let's get rid of it."'

From February onwards the pace of change grew hotter and hotter. Politically, one result of the Brussels conference was that the Governor-General created a College of six Commissioners (who included Kasavubu and Lumumba) in nominal control of major departments of the administration, in an effort at a crash programme to teach responsibility to some of the obvious future leaders. This was inaugurated on 14 March, Kasavubu with the Finance portfolio: he had been a clerk in that department for many years. The system worked after a fashion, but was vitiated by the fact that there was no kind of collective responsibility; and ultimate power rested wholly with the Governor-General. Nevertheless, these six Commissioners put in a hard day's work. Once when Lumumba was dining with us, I asked him how many hours sleep he succeeded in getting each night. At this time he was not only doing his job with the Governor-General but at the same time desperately trying to create an all-Congo political party. He replied that he spent his day in his government office and then returned home to find anything from thirty to sixty people waiting to see him. He dealt with them until about 11 or 12 at night and then started his party office and organizational work until 2 or 3 o'clock in the morning. He had to get up early to see other visitors and averaged therefore between two and three hours' sleep. This was an impossible intensity; and yet he had to live like this because he belonged to merely a small tribe, mainly inhabitants of Orientale province (although he himself had been born in north Kasai), and thus his only hope of achieving the position of a leader was to create from nothing an all-Congo political party which would attract support from all the six provinces, cutting across the tribal loyalties on which most of his competitors relied. And he only had three months in which to do it.

Administratively, too, a crash programme was attempted. There was no Congolese who could pretend to be appointed to Grade 1 of the administration, but some hundreds were promoted into higher grades from the four bottom grades. Special training courses were arranged and a number of Congolese were sent to Belgium for study and training. Time was so short that there was clearly no possibility of this working out by the date of Independence; and, as the difficulties multiplied, the wildest stories soon began to circulate as to what sort of administration would then be functioning. Action was also taken in the six provinces to set up, in parallel with the new College of Commissioners at the centre, similar nominated advisory councils of leading Congolese to work with each of the Provincial Governors and so try to learn something of the administration they were about to inherit.

The ordinary Congolese is a credulous and fearful person. Bomboko, who later became the country's first, and is its present, Foreign Minister, told me one day that Europeans would never understand Africans because they were so different. He himself was one of scarcely a dozen Congolese university graduates; more than that, he had taught for one term in a college in Belgium. He said that when he was a boy and had to go at night from his house across the courtyard to another room, he ran with his mouth wide open, screaming, in order to keep the evil spirits away. The fear of the unknown was never far below the surface. Against that kind of psychology it was small wonder that the bids offered by political parties grew wilder and wilder. In one area the people were told that they should sit at the graves of their forefathers on Independence Day and see them rise from the dead—provided of course that they voted for a particular candidate. A Belgian lady told us that the tailor who came to work for her on her verandah said quite casually in conversation one day that he had bought her and her sewing-machine as from the date of Independence. She asked what on earth he meant; and he repeated his statement adding that there was a man in town who was selling European wives for ten shillings each. Needless to say, this lady and her family made one of the early pre-Independence departures from the Congo.

Professor van Bilsen lunched with us one day. His is a great name in the history of the Congo because he had both understanding of and sympathy with the desire for independence. He was particularly interesting to us about Kasavubu, whom he knew well. I said that I got the impression that people did not know what Kasavubu meant to do: they were not sure whether he had renounced his ideas of a Bakongo state, independent of the rest of the Congo and perhaps including parts of Angola and of the French Congo (which did not become fully independent until some weeks later than the Belgian colony) across the river. I had the feeling that people were not certain that he had put his heart into the idea of the Belgian Congo as a future independent entity. Professor van Bilsen replied that this was in Kasavubu's character. He was an introverted, solitary person. Van Bilsen had lately talked with two schoolmates of Kasavubu who said that he was the same at school— independent and turned in on himself; he had a tremendous feeling for tradition and the past. Van Bilsen thought that he *had* accepted the unitary Congo idea now. When the idea of a Bakongo state had been mooted, it was because the rest of the Congo had then been lagging behind, which was not the case now. The Bakongo were the fighters for independence and they felt that they should not be tied to the rest of the Congo if this was resented. Kasavubu was now planning, so Professor van Bilsen said, a tour of the whole Congo, and he also wished to get the other Congolese leaders from elsewhere in the country to come to the Bakongo and show themselves. I asked why in that case he had not come out openly with such a policy. He had refrained from making a public declaration about it, and people were wondering, for example, why he had been the only one of the College of Six who had not applauded the Governor-General's speech when the College was formally inaugurated. Van Bilsen said that he was still suspicious. At the Round Table Conference in Brussels he had gone away because he did not trust the Belgians: he thought then that even when they gave a date for Independence they would take it back again. About that time the date for Cyprus Independence had been put off and Kasavubu had said, 'There—you see? They just agreed on a date to get these people disarmed and then they cancelled it.' This suspiciousness of Kasavubu continued. For example, said van Bilsen, he had a proposal put before him by a group of international financiers about the development of the

Inga project, which was a scheme for the harnessing of the hydro-electric power of the Congo river. He was asked to sign the proposal at once so that plans could go ahead. Kasavubu refused, because he did not understand the documents involved; this was partly because of his character and partly because of his suspicion that those concerned were playing a trick on him, and that they were hoping to retain by economic agreements the hold on the Congo which the Belgian government were giving away in the political conference. Lumumba, van Bilsen said, was quite different: he would happily have signed the agreement, saying that if he did not like it in three months' time he would unsign.

I asked how an introverted person like Kasavubu could acquire such influence. Van Bilsen said that the Bakongo tribe had been educated by Flemish Roman Catholics who, without realizing it, had passed on the Flemish attitude of being 'agin the government'—a minority in Belgium, resentful of the French-speaking majority's monopoly of power. He said that there was quite a parallel between the Flemish and the Bakongo situation, and awareness of this had helped to make the Bakongo tribally and culturally self-conscious. They looked back to their own proud history and Kasavubu was deeply steeped in it. Van Bilsen, who has travelled widely in Africa, said that he believed that in British and French colonies and ex-colonies there was more feeling of friendship for the ruling colonial power than in the Congo, because of the education which they had received and the fact that so many had studied in Britain and France. Van Bilsen could not unfortunately stay permanently in the Congo as he had to return to his post in the college in Belgium which trained administrators for the Congo. That, however, he remarked, would soon be ended. I inquired whether it was intended to transfer the college to the Congo for the benefit of the Congolese administrators. But van Bilsen said that that was not proposed. He added with a smile that one year previously there had been talk of dismissing him because of an article which he had written in 1956—a plan for Congolese independence after thirty years. How could anyone be induced, so his critics had said, to join the Belgian administrative services in the Congo if they thought that the country would be independent before the end of their careers? A Belgian Minister had himself ridiculed the idea in public speeches, which read oddly when the same Minister visited the Congo in early 1960 and spoke an entirely different language. It was, however, too late, he said, to change the outlook of the generation of Belgians who were then in the Congo.

We early made the acquaintance of a young Belgian professor of economics in the University, and his wife. He was an able and devoted teacher, liked and trusted by the Congolese and in full sympathy with the demand for independence. As time went on he did not spare himself in giving the Congolese all the help he could to working out economic plans and in providing financial and economic advice. The situation soon began to show signs of strain, although, economically, as the weeks before Independence passed, there was not much outward evidence of a reduction in activity. The Congo is a very rich country with many valuable minerals; it produced at that time seventy per cent of the world's industrial diamonds as well as the famous Katanga copper. The Hiroshima bomb had been made, so it was said, with Congo uranium; the gold in the Orientale province was a useful export; and there were valuable deposits of cobalt and manganese. Kivu province had enormous areas suitable for large-scale plantation farming and could produce as high quality crops as the Kenya highlands. Unilever alone gave employment, direct or indirect, to many tens of thousands on palm-oil plantations and in a soap and margarine factory in Léopoldville. The firm also had in Léopoldville, incidentally, the largest self-service store which my wife and I had at that time ever seen; and it was very well stocked.

The young professor was worried about the financial situation at the time of Independence. There would be no ready money available but only a large debt for the Congo to start life with. It would be a problem even for the government to be able to pay salaries to its administration. Well before the date of Independence the government began to delay payment of bills to a number of firms; and for the small man and the café the habit grew of a new and enlarged Congolese clientele signing chits for supplies but not paying. In most cases the proprietor felt that he could not risk refusing to do business on this basis.

As time went on, a change came over the spirit of the people. In the hot, humid weeks of April and early May, the end of the rainy season, a ground-swell of doubt began. An increasing exodus of Belgian families took place. The men mostly stayed, except for those going on holiday; but by the month of May the Belgian airline Sabena was running an extra seventy Boeing flights a month out of Léopoldville. No one reason, except just fear of the unknown, was given for this. The Belgians in the Congo were hard-headed realists; they had created an administration which was competent and just, paternal certainly, and perhaps harsh sometimes. They loved their work and many had a sense of mission in the Congo. Independence was a sudden new concept; and they lacked the flexibility and the pragmatic approach to new relationships which have marked the British in many such situations. But there were many and varied individual reasons, apart from an unpreparedness to face the unknown. Even some university staff who had been a long time in the Congo would say that they had been accustomed to speak down to all blacks—to '*tutoyer*' them—and they could not accept the change. 'We were good to them; but we used to go ahead of them in a queue and now we can't face calling them "*Monsieur*" and waiting behind them.' And in some of the remoter areas it had been only a year or two previously that the whipping of plantation workers had finally died out: some of those Belgian settlers were perhaps wise to get out and justified in feeling apprehensive.

As the British representative in the Congo I was also Consul-General for the Belgian-administered territory of Ruanda-Urundi, formerly a German colony but mandated to Belgium after the First World War for the obvious reason that its administration could best be run in parallel with that of the neighbouring Congo. It was unlikely that I would have the chance later, so I took the opportunity in the spring of 1960, before the Congo elections, to make a rapid tour of the country. I went by air to Usumbura, the capital, which lies at the northern end of Lake Tanganyika. I hired a taxi there and covered some six hundred miles in a week. I stayed with Belgian officials and the Protestant bishop and also in hotels. I met and talked with as many people as I could, and felt that when I came away I had got at any rate an impression of what was going on—and of what was in store.

The basic fact about Ruanda-Urundi was that fifteen per cent of the people belonged to the tall Watutsi, Nilotic people, fine-featured and intelligent; and eighty-five per cent were Bahutu, or Bantu, similar in physique to most of the Africans of Central and Southern Africa. For some hundreds of years the Watutsi had ruled the country—they were the land-owners and the herd-owners, as well as the country's leaders. The Bahutu were the serfs and the peasants. It was rare for one of the Watutsi to be seen doing any manual labour, and common on the other hand for Watutsi women to be carried in a kind of palanquin. As long as Belgium exercised its overlordship and did not seem to be giving up its authority this system continued without much trouble. But the wind of change blew here too; and as soon as the realization spread that the Belgians were going, the struggle for the inheritance of power began.

This not only took the form of hit-and-run raids by the one community on the other in the marginal areas where there was a small minority living among a large majority—this was of course usually the case with a group of Watutsi living among the Bahutu—but it also spread into lobbying at the United Nations, then perhaps in its heyday of Afro-Asian emotion. As a result of this latter circumstance, a Commission was set up, under the chairmanship of a Liberian woman, to consider the future of Ruanda-Urundi. In due course this Commission reported, as could have been foreseen before it began, that Ruanda-Urundi should immediately become independent with the one-man one-vote type of democracy which was all that the U.N. was prepared to consider or that entered into its calculations.

It was obvious that catastrophe must ensue. This is not written with hindsight and I may be permitted to quote from a letter which I wrote to the Foreign Office in March 1962 (some time after I had ceased to have any connection with Congo affairs) as follows:

I cannot refrain from adding my own personal view, based on some knowledge of Ruanda–Urundi affairs, that it will be folly for the General Assembly to vote for the independence of this country on 1 July. I should like H.M.G. to say, loud out, that that would be an irresponsible act with which we refuse to associate ourselves; and that we shall decline to bear any of the subsequent costs of dealing with events. These costs should be put squarely on to those who insist on incurring them by voting for such a resolution. I gave my ideas on Ruanda–Urundi's future in a despatch from Léopoldville in April 1960; some of them may perhaps still be relevant.

The personal views which I had earlier expressed were to the effect that there could not fail to be mutual massacre of Bahutu and Watutsi if independence were introduced without warning. No heed, however, was paid to such representations—indeed I never even had an acknow-ledgement of my letter; and Ruanda-Urundi not only became indepen-dent a few months later but became two independent countries, Rwanda and Burundi, having been first sliced in half. This seems to me still, as it did then, the most shameful single thing the U.N. has ever done. What was then still called Ruanda-Urundi is a beautiful country, lying, in the main, in an altitude between three and five thousand feet, with rolling hills and a not unpleasant climate; it is intensely cultivated. It is a poor country, lost in the middle of Africa; but with its physical location and the Mountains of the Moon on its north-western edge, as well as a string of lakes north from Lake Tanganyika, it could have been one of the great tourist and holiday resorts of Africa and the world.

But the fetish of democratic freedom decreed otherwise. If the result was going to be that a few people would be massacred, or even a few hundred, maybe this could have been justified on the grounds that good government could be no substitute for self-government. But when it was a case of thousands being butchered and tens of thousands forced to become refugees in neighbouring countries, while hundreds of thousands lived in fear at home, I cannot believe that, on any rational computation of right and wrong, it was right for the U.N. to take the action which it did. It would have been feasible for a standing committee of the U.N. to be set up to advise the Belgian administration on the steps which they should take for the gradual education of the people and their association with the processes of government. But it is only to be condemned when theoretical decisions, taken in many cases on grounds of irrational prejudices by people whom the decision did not directly concern, caused such misery to so many others.

The right course would have been for a Belgian trusteeship to have continued, with such oversight as might have been either considered necessary or desirable, for an unlimited number of years. The division of the country into two, neither of which has a Watutsi majority, was made in order to create a better balance of the races in one of the two resulting countries. This left the Watutsi in the other one in the fearful position of hostages. But the change was too sudden and the natural supports for self-government too lacking for the experiment to have any chance of success. Few people now give a thought to the way in which life continues in Rwanda and Burundi, or to the terrible consequences through the years for the victims of the racist obsessions of those living comfortably thousands of miles away.

A sad victim of this political evolution was the weakening, in Ruanda-Urundi as in the Congo, of INEAC. I urged, before Independence of the Congo, that this first-class agricultural research organization, created by the Belgians in both the Congo and Ruanda-Urundi, should be internationalized with the help of the U.N. and expanded into a body serving all tropical Africa in one of its most vital needs. There were thousands of acres in experimental use, and some four hundred Belgian scientists were doing most valuable work with teams of a thousand Congolese. It was dispiriting to look forward to the breakup of this fine body of men and experience; and it could so easily have been transformed and enlarged. I never got any reply or comment from any source on my proposals. In the brief fifteen months before I left the Congo, the scientists had gone and the jungle was returning.

3

Elections were duly held all over the Congo from 11 to 25 May, followed by the election on 9 June by the Provincial Assemblies of their quota of senators to the Upper Chamber at the centre. Parties formed, broke up, and realigned with kaleidoscopic speed in the weeks immediately before the election. Forty Belgian magistrates were brought out to supervise the process, which took place against a background of a steady and visible crumbling of the administration. It was not only that the local administration was unable to function satisfactorily—in parts of Léopoldville province the Bakongo set up a parallel government and the legal one could not even collect taxes or ensure the functioning of the courts. In Kasai province a bitter tribal war went on even in and around its capital, Luluabourg, which I visited at the end of April. I saw hundreds of abandoned huts, convoys of refugees, and actually witnessed a minor clash in the middle of the city. By then, so the local army commander told me, 140 corpses had been picked up by the police and various parts of human bodies were still being found. Ambushes, murder, and mutilation began to be common during the first half of 1960 as the Lulua and Baluba tribes took steps to separate out from each other's localities.

In Stanleyville, the capital of Orientale province, inter-tribal fighting also began the very day when the Governor-General, accompanied by his six African members of the College of Commissioners, arrived on a visit. Lumumba stayed behind for some weeks to organize his party for the election in that province when the others returned to Léopoldville. Lumumba conducted a campaign with strong overtones of violence in the city of Stanleyville and in Orientale province; and an abortive attempt was made to seize power there by a coup d'état. Troops had to be called out in force one night on the orders of the Governor and his African Councillors in order to safeguard the main buildings in the city. Lumumba alarmed the Europeans in Orientale during this three-week campaign by fostering xenophobia and—perhaps with some reason— he accused a number of Belgian officials of working against him. He complained to the Pope about the activities of some of the Belgian priests in the province, and sharply attacked the Commander-in-Chief of the Force Publique, the Congolese Army, for denouncing intimidation and terrorism as a means of winning the election. Finally he resigned from the Governor-General's Council, ostensibly in protest at Belgian attitudes and actions (such as bringing a few more troops to the Congo) but no doubt in reality to leave himself free to devote himself entirely to the elections and subsequent political manoeuvring. Lumumba had alarmed many Congolese political leaders in the meanwhile and his colleagues on the Governor-General's Council, who strongly criticized both the kind of propaganda which he had been making and the intemperate language he had been using. This had some effect in persuading Lumumba that perhaps, even in his own interests, he had over-reached himself and jeopardized his chances of subsequently leading a coalition government. He then began to exert all his influence to calm down a situation which he had himself inflamed. The danger, then as on many subsequent occasions, was that while it was easy to stir up credulous people to frenzied action, quite different qualities were required to ride the subsequent storm. Even Anicet Kashamura, that most lightweight of all the Congo politicians, felt that Lumumba had gone too far, and abandoned him in order to resume his own seat on the Governor-General's Council which he had resigned along with Lumumba.

Apart from the trouble in Kasai and Orientale provinces, in Léopoldville itself there were forty political murders in the African sections of the city before the elections were over. Despite all this, however, which was a by-product of tribal feeling and the ruthless pursuit of the struggle for power by some of the Congolese leaders, the elections went on all over the country. There was a heightening of fear and tension in many places both among Europeans and Africans; and daylight murders continued even in the capital, mainly among members of the two warring Kasai tribes, Lulua and Baluba, who lived there. A curfew had to be imposed on 13 May in one African commune and was extended the next day to all the African areas. The army, under its forceful Commander-in-Chief, began to demand the right to take over some, at any rate, of the control of law and order. The Belgian authorities hung back on this proposal, even though the Congolese members of the Governor-General's Council were prepared to support it. Partly, perhaps, this result was due to the unfortunate fact that at this juncture the Governor-General and Commander-in-Chief did not see eye to eye. Another proposal which failed was for the immediate installation of a provisional government, partly in order that a Congolese Minister should have responsibility for the security situation. It was difficult to see how this could have been done: it was already too late for the Belgians to take back or exercise full power. The time-table for the transfer of power was short and exacting and could not be changed in a matter of weeks before Independence was due. Deplorable and painful as the position was in so many respects, it could perhaps have been argued that all this was a necessary stage in the process of accelerated political evolution which the sudden granting of independence had forced on the Congo. If indeed this period could have been turned to advantage by bringing home to Congolese leaders, even for the short time remaining before Independence, the problems of maintaining law and order as the basis of any administration (and they were becoming well aware of the need for such a basis), then the experiences which everyone was enduring might have produced some positive result. This was not to be, however, and the Congolese had to learn a harder way.

The elections came to an end and produced the results shown in the

Election Results for Legislative Assembly

Mouvement National Congolais (M.N.C./Lumumba)	33
Parti National du Progrès (P.N.P.) (Reko, ARP, Mederco, Luka, Front Commun)	19
Parti Solidaire Africain (P.S.A.)	13
Alliance des Bakongo (Abako)	12
Centre de Regroupement Africain (Cerea)	9
Confédération des Associations Tribales du Katanga (Conakat)	8
Mouvement National Congolais (M.N.C./Kalonji)	8
Parti d'Unité Nationale (Puna)	7
Cartel Balubakat	6
Independents	5
Union Nationale Congolaise	3
Association Ngwaka (Puna)	2
Coalition Kasaienne (Coaka)	2
Local interests	2
Cerea/Kashamura	1
Union des Mongos (Unimo)	1
Alliance des Bayazi (Abazi)	1
R.D.L.K.	1
Atcar (Cartel Balubakat)	1
Cartel M.U.B./M.N.C. Lumumba	1
Cartel Coaka/M.N.C. Lumumba	1
UNEBAFI/M.N.C. Lumumba	1

The results are interesting mainly for showing the strength of Lumumba's party, with 33 seats in the wing led by Lumumba aud eight in Kalonji's (restricted to the Balubas of Kasai). Secondly, they show the proliferation of parties (and initials—a Belgian legacy) which had no lasting significance but gave great scope for political manoeuvring.

table. Lumumba's party, the M.N.C., was the largest, though split—significantly—into two wings: one under himself and the other led by Kalonji, the Baluba leader in Kasai. There had been some cases of intimidation, burning of ballot boxes, attacks on returning officers, and so on, during the two weeks the elections had lasted. But by and large the results were accepted as reflecting the opinion of the voters. There was anyhow no time to hear election petitions or complaints—by the time the results were out Independence was only five weeks away. The law-and-order situation by the end of May had temporarily stabilized at a low level, except for continued tribal warfare in parts of Kasai.

So had the state of the country's economy. For many months past this had been going through a difficult and bleak period: the ordinary budget was running a deficit, the extraordinary or capital budget was in heavy deficit, reserves were exhausted, and remittances abroad subject to a series of controls which, however necessary, were by then mainly an irritant and largely unproductive as the big money had already left the country. Central and provincial governments were months in arrears with the payment of their bills; and this kind of situation obtained in all fields of the economy. The staff of Lovanium University, for example, received their pay increasingly in arrears. The Vice-Governor-General told me that the Congo was running on a hand-to-mouth basis and that he did not know—financially speaking—what would happen after 30 June. This was therefore the situation facing the Congolese politicians after the elections, and it was complicated by the intimation from the Association of Civil Servants that they proposed all to go on strike at the end of May if their demands concerning remittances to Belgium and re-integration in the Belgian civil service were not met in full. They had seen the big companies send their millions back to Belgium and now found themselves unable to send their hundreds or thousands.

Into this disturbed situation Ganshof van der Meersch had come from Belgium as a specially appointed resident Minister to deal with the last weeks of colonial rule. He had been faced at once with the resignations of Lumumba and Kashamura from the Governor-General's Council: this was partly in protest at his own appointment. It was clear that a government of national unity was needed because no one party had won sufficient seats in the election to enable it to rule by itself; but still more because without experience all round in the arts of government, it would not be desirable to have even a coalition of parties to rule if they could count on making up only a bare majority of the votes. That would imply that those left out would be content to be a loyal opposition in the Westminster tradition of parliamentary democracy. But loyalty to a system which was totally alien was of course non-existent. Lumumba saw this need for a national coalition, and tried to a considerable extent to meet it. But he failed.

Partly this was due to Belgian activities. Understandably, the Belgians were dismayed at the prospect of Lumumba's becoming the Prime Minister of the new Congo; they had hoped for someone whom they felt they could trust. But that does not excuse the manoeuvres of the next fortnight following the elections. Lumumba had secured overwhelming support in his own Orientale province. He had 33 members of the 137 in the central legislature, and support of varying degree in the provinces both from his own party members and from persons who were prepared to accept his leadership. Nowhere, however, except in the Orientale provincial assembly, did he command an outright majority.

Then began a period of intense party and individual manoeuvring. Lumumba issued a statement on 1 June to the effect that he should be called upon to form the central government. He denounced the 'climate of uneasiness and insecurity which runs everywhere' and alleged that the Belgian authorities were trying to form a coalition to keep him out of power. He added that his party wished for friendship between all races and tribes and recognized the need for a 'European presence in the Congo'. The independence of the Congo was to be 'for the benefit of all the inhabitants, black and white', and the future State would look forward to assistance from 'all the friends of liberty and of Africa'. Finally, the statement demanded:

(i) The immediate withdrawal of the Belgian troops who had recently come to the Congo;

(ii) The immediate return to Belgium of Ganshof van der Meersch;

(iii) The election of the future Head of State by universal suffrage—this was in effect to ask for a Lumumba nominee;

(iv) The formation of the future central government by the party which had won the largest number of seats; and

(v) A new national flag, other than the one which had been devised with the help of the Belgians.

Lumumba was right, as I was told on the highest authority, in his allegations of Belgian machinations to keep him out of power, but, try as they might, the Belgians could not succeed. They only delayed the decision and embittered Lumumba further. Uncertainty, infirmity of purpose, and lack of clear leadership at this time continued the process of general overall disintegration. If things could not go smoothly and sensibly at the centre, what hopes were there out in the provinces? Inside Kasai province a group of missionaries were told by the Baluba tribesmen, among whom they lived, that they should go away by 30 June. This, it was made clear, was not because there was anything against them but because the tribe intended to settle, once and for all, its troubles with the Lulua; and no one, they said, not even the Congolese Army, was going to be allowed to get in the way of this wholesale settlement of accounts. And such were the consequences of a sophisticated political structure being imposed on an immature people that, in four out of the six provinces, defeated parties were threatening secession because they would not accept the idea that they should have no power, and because the victors showed no sign of the necessary restraint and generosity in dealing with the losers in the elections. These parties (except Lumumba's) being essentially tribal groupings, sometimes strong and well led, it was an obvious necessity that room be found in the hierarchy of power for leaders of all the major parties, as no great tribe would agree to be ruled by another. Some of the leaders realized this and the consequent need for coalition governments in the provinces; but by no means all had this awareness. The Congo was not at a stage of political development when it could afford the luxury of a strong opposition either at the centre or in any of the provinces.

As late as 10 June, with three weeks to go to Independence, the Governor-General told me that he did not think Lumumba would become the head of the Congo government. This was despite all the evidence of Lumumba's skill as a political manipulator, organizer, and compelling speaker. A small example of Lumumba's unscrupulous political adroitness is perhaps worth recording as an illustration of his character. Fearing the way which the election would go in Kasai province, where the Kalonji wing of his M.N.C. party consisted wholly of the Baluba tribe, Lumumba already in April had made private agreements with leaders of smaller parties and independent candidates in Kasai. When the provincial election gave Kalonji one-third of the seats, though that was the same proportion as Lumumba's wing of the party had obtained at the centre, which formed the basis of Lumumba's claim to the Prime Ministership of the Congo, Lumumba made use of his previously arranged agreements and refused to back Kalonji to be Prime Minister of Kasai province. This inevitably caused resentment and resulted in a Baluba threat to secede; and in fact in a few months Kalonji had set up a separate state, based on the Baluba tribe. Perhaps Lumumba had not been so clever after all.

In the same way Lumumba manoeuvred at the centre and forced the Belgians to call on him on 13 June, as the *'Informateur'* to Ganshof van der Meersch, to report on whether a government of national unity could be formed. Then on 17 June, as Lumumba had not succeeded, partly because a fortnight's delay in calling on him had eroded his position and encouraged others, Kasavubu was appointed *'Formateur'*. This was a step nearer to heading a government than merely reporting about the possible formation of a government. Kasavubu failed in his assignment. I do not believe that his heart was in it, as he wanted to be Head of State, a position for which he was much more suited by temperament and character. On 21 June Ganshof van der Meersch again called on Lumumba, this time as *'Formateur'*. After much jockeying for position, Lumumba formed his Cabinet of 23 Ministers, four Ministers of State, and ten Secretaries of State; and Kasavubu was duly elected Head of State. Lumumba's government included members of all the major tribes and parties, with the notable exception of the Baluba of Kasai. Many politicians, however, were disappointed and this was reflected in the vote of confidence which the new government obtained on 23 June. Only three-fifths of the members of the Lower House attended, one of whom only voted against Lumumba's government. The following day in the Senate Lumumba obtained a majority of 60 to 12 with 8 abstentions. This therefore was the government with which the Congo reached Independence.

The voting procedures during those few meetings of the Congo Parliament before Independence had all gone smoothly. Indeed, the very first meeting had been encouraging. The galleries were full and the body of the Chamber was occupied by the elected representatives, some in their tribal dress but the vast majority in ordinary suits. Good-humour and the ritual of similar assemblies elsewhere produced the effect, as unexpected as it was in its way impressive, that maybe this strangely and suddenly imported system would work. Could it really be that power could be transferred so smoothly? What was the reality behind the appearances? Those elected representatives had had no experience of working together before. The Congo utterly lacked the vast variety of voluntary associations which alone can guarantee that political association has a solid basis on which to rest; the new body had no new muscles—would the old ones go on functioning with new blood and with a new nervous system?

4

Perhaps at this point in the story of the Congo one should take a look further back. Just over half a century earlier, as General Janssens had outlined to myself and my wife, King Léopold II had induced a reluctant Belgium to take over the vast estate in Central Africa which his vision and determination had created. Having followed with passionate interest the discoveries of Livingstone and Stanley, he used Stanley from 1878 onwards to explore and build up the territory until it was recognized by the Conference of Berlin in 1884 as a sovereign state under his absolute rule. Then for nearly a quarter of a century this '*géant dans un cave*' drove his agents to develop the country, sometimes by means which aroused the horror of the civilized world.

Thus it was that only in 1908 did the Congo begin its short but remarkable colonial career, during which the country became an ever more profitable field of investment for Belgium and was transformed into what was in some respects a model colony. Endowed by nature with great mineral wealth, including copper, diamonds, gold, manganese, cobalt, and uranium, with vast areas suitable for the cultivation of palm oil, rubber, cotton, and coffee, the Congo prospered exceedingly under the orderly administration which the Belgians established. Although in theory it was part of the Free Trade Zone set up by the Berlin Conference of 1884–5 for all the world to trade with and invest in, the lion's share of the benefit inevitably accrued to Belgium, which by the time of Independence had investments in the country totalling far over £1,000 million. The ordinary budget of the state balanced at about £110 million per year; its exports and re-exports for the year 1959 (according to the Bulletin of the Central Bank) were £175 million, and imports £108 million. This was one measure of Belgium's economic development of the country in the half-century. An integrated system of communications had been developed, economically devised so as to use thousands of miles of navigable river where possible and rail and road only where these were necessary. Regular through-passenger rail, road, and steamer services covered the main routes throughout the country. The agricultural potential had been studied and developed through excellent research institutes and by heavy investment, for example by Unilever in palm-oil plantations. A steadily expanding secondary industry had grown up, particularly in the ten years preceding Independence; there were by 1960 a number of large cities with modern amenities of life—Léopoldville had become one of the finest modern cities in Africa; and the standard of living of the African urban population was high.

In concentrating on orderly administration, impartial justice, economic development, and social welfare, the Belgians thought that they had found the solution for Africa. Mainly through missionary enterprise, primary education was fairly widespread; and technical education had advanced rapidly, particularly in the major mining and smelting areas of Katanga province. The department of African housing had built 40,000 brick houses in Léopoldville alone; and comprehensive social legislation looked after health services, pensions, and family allowances. While providing in these ways for the material well-being of the Congolese, the Belgians deliberately withheld from them the opportunities for higher education which would have fitted them one day to govern themselves. Thus it was only in 1958 that the first Congolese student was allowed to begin the study of law; and while there were tens of thousands of skilled and semi-skilled artisans there was not as yet one Congolese doctor, engineer, or army officer; and not one Congolese girl with enough education to enter a university. There were in all only a dozen or so Congolese graduates from foreign universities: they had achieved their education in spite of Belgian discouragement, for officially, until very shortly before Independence, only studies for the priesthood had been allowed abroad.

There is no doubt that if Belgium had had another twenty-five years, with no political nervousness to deter increasing capital investment, the Congo as a whole might well have achieved a prosperity and a standard of living higher than any other country in Africa, with the possible exception of the Republic of South Africa. As late as 1956 official thinking was outraged at the idea produced by van Bilsen (as he had told us himself) of a thirty-year plan to lead the Congo to independence.

It may well be asked why the Congolese demand for independence suddenly grew so powerful that the Belgians were compelled to take urgent notice of it. There were perhaps three things which mainly contributed to this, apart from the general ferment in Africa from which the Belgians mistakenly thought the Congo could be isolated. The first had been General de Gaulle's famous speech, on his visit to Brazzaville in August 1958, which gave the French territories on the other side of the Congo river the right to decide their own future. The fact that the kind of independence then envisaged involved the closest economic ties with France—of a kind which would have been called neo-colonialist if they had not been so indispensable—was not understood in the Belgian Congo. The message that came across was this spectacular new conception (new to this particular part of Africa) that the European rulers were handing over power; the effect on the Congolese was instantaneous and produced within two days a petition to the Governor-General for the same right of determination.

The second important event was the Brussels World Fair of 1958, when one of the principal exhibits had been a Congolese village with some hundreds of Congolese brought over for the occasion to Belgium and housed in their traditional huts. These human exhibits, for that is in fact what they were, dressed the part, gave their tribal music and dances, and showed off their way of life. This in one sense advertised the Congo; but for the hundreds of Congolese involved it rapidly rebounded into a feeling of resentment at being treated and shown off like strange animals. The Fair went on long enough for the impact of this to be widely and deeply felt, and to be taken back to the Congo. Other results from that event also contributed: the Congolese saw the sort of life which ordinary people lived in Brussels; and they found, too, that white prostitutes did not practise any colour bar. This brought many back to the Congo with a new kind of outlook and produced a restless dissatisfaction with the old shut-in way of life. Only a very few carefully selected Congolese had ever previously been allowed to leave the country for travel or education abroad. It was at this Fair, too, that the Belgian Communist Party made its first contacts with Congolese. Back in Léopoldville, by December 1958, four major political groups had established themselves.

The third event, important mainly to Lumumba personally, was the All-African Peoples Conference held in Accra in December 1958 which Lumumba and leaders of two other political groups in the Congo attended. Nkrumah dominated this meeting; and it not only inspired Lumumba to sharpen demands for independence but opened his eyes to the possibilities for himself of becoming a great leader in the fight for African freedom. Kasavubu had been prevented by the Belgians from attending the Conference because, ironically enough, they then regarded him as a more dangerous nationalist leader than Lumumba, since he had already for some years been politically active in the Lower Congo.

Why, next, after refusing to contemplate or prepare for such a change, did Belgium so suddenly decide to grant total independence to the Congo at such very short notice? I asked this of many but never got a satisfactory answer; and probably there is no sufficient single reason. The most generally accepted explanation was that the Congo was a plaything of Belgian internal politics. The Congo was Belgium's one and only colony and eighty-nine times the size of Belgium (curiously, with the same length of coastline as Belgium itself). Belgium had not wanted the colony in the first instance and had only very reluctantly been persuaded by Léopold II to take over the Congo, when it was clearly turning into a very good business proposition. And Belgium is a small European state which had itself existed, in a fairly uneasy political union internally, for a bare half-century before Léopold II began his African adventure.

There were many in Belgium who still did not want a colony at all. Experiences, for example, of Belgians on leave from the Congo, driving about Belgium with Congolese number-plates on their cars, bore this out. Several had told us, during the voyage to Matadi, of coming out of country restaurants in Belgium to find a hostile group round their car, and even on occasion of being stoned—presumably through jealousy of their better-paid jobs as well as dislike of the idea of being involved in a colonial enterprise. Thus many of the Belgian people at home had neither understanding for, nor any wish to be involved with, a colony in Africa once it became apparent that it would cost them either money or the opprobrium in the United Nations Organization which the use of force against a political independence movement would have brought upon them. The British were accustomed to attacks in the world's press and in the U.N. for being colonialists and suppressing freedom movements. We could afford to pay no attention to these (or not much) but, the Belgians explained, they could not. They were not prepared to incur the odium, as it seemed to them, and the obloquy.

The shock produced by the Léopoldville riots of January 1959 was all the greater because the Belgians genuinely believed until then that theirs was the one really well-behaved colony in Africa. When they found that it was not so, they were thrown back into their former suspicion of the whole colonial business. They did not know how to deal with an incipient nationalist movement and alternated between half-hearted attempts at repression and unthinking appeasement. The result was to create suspicion both of Belgium's intentions and of its political capacity. I had never before heard nationals of any country declare themselves (as several Belgians did to me in different parts of the Congo) ashamed to belong to their country. And both the head of the Central Bank and a local judge said to me that they were 'disgusted' at the way Belgium had lately been handling Congo affairs. The risk for the Congo of the sudden transition to independence was certainly great; and one can only imagine that there were certain limitations to the Belgian way of thinking that led the Belgians to believe that, by granting all political requests whenever they were made, they would be able to stay on, run the country under a Congolese Ministry, and go on enjoying the economic fruits of their exploitation of the Congo (which was what mainly interested them). To such an extent does that attitude seem to have been predominant that the sudden Congolese demand at the Brussels conference to bring the date of Independence forward from the end of July to the end of June was readily agreed.

If the gamble had come off, then the vast Belgian investments in the Congo—worth over £1,000 million at the time, apart from prospecting rights—would of course have been saved; and the economy would have functioned as before. To what extent the decisions of the government in Brussels were influenced by pressures from big business, I had no means of knowing, but it was widely believed that they were. The Roman Catholic Church, too, with its four thousand Belgian priests and nuns in the Congo, must clearly have made its views heard in Brussels—to what purpose, again, I am unable even to speculate. Public opinion in Brussels was divided and perplexed; and this was reflected in government actions and decisions.

The Belgians did not play their hand skilfully; and by seeking to keep too much of the economic benefits to themselves they risked losing more of them than they need otherwise have lost. And by their obvious support of certain political parties and leaders in the Congo, by the intrigues of big business and certain intellectuals (such as members of the staff of the Institut Solvay), they sowed distrust of their motives which they could with difficulty live down. In their association with the Congo, indeed, nothing became the Belgians so little as their manner of leaving it.

5

By the time of Independence therefore, despite the complexity of the
Congo's tribal structure and the lack of experience among its leaders,
the absence of any unifying programme or outlook, the vacillations of
Belgian policy, and, it must be said, the machinations of many Belgians,
a political settlement had been reached, with a government of national
union in office. Lumumba had shown notable skill in organizing the
formation of his national government; and Kasavubu's election as
Head of State had given the Congo as good and as acceptable a father-
figure as was possible. There were also, however, an empty treasury
and a heavy accumulation of public debt; there were pitifully few educated persons in the whole country, where the ignorance and credulity
of the people made it difficult for principles or larger ideas to overcome
tribal loyalties. There was little feeling of nationalism or patriotism
among the many tribes who inhabited the vast area of the Congo. It was
already clear that provincial boundaries would have to be retraced; but
it was one thing to contemplate evolving gradually in that direction with
a central authority to exercise overall control—it was quite another to
try to force the pace at once, which could only have the effect of disastrously weakening the centre. Another major difficulty was that
Belgium had provided the new Congo with a constitution embodying
a complicated system of proportional representation, which few could
understand, and a nice division of powers between the Head of State
and the Cabinet, which was not an African formula. 'What the Congo
needed,' as I had reported towards the end of June, 'in the African
rather than the European tradition, is one executive Head of Government who is known and can be seen to be a leader.' Instead of this, a
bicameral legislature had been created which was certain to prove
frustrating in practice, all the more so as the Upper Chamber had
very considerable powers. The Congo needed 'a strong government of
national unity both to pull the country together and to plan its development'; for there was no doubt that the state would have to play a leading
role in the direction of the economy, if the balanced development of
agriculture and industry and the introduction of new techniques to

backward areas and primitive peoples were to be quickly and successfully accomplished.

There were those who placed their hopes in the Congolese Army (the Force Publique as it had been called in Belgian days) as a strong unifying influence—the only one—in the Congo. It is therefore perhaps worth while to give a short account of its origins and history. It had been established by King Léopold II at Boma, near the mouth of the Congo river, in 1886; and it consisted at first of mainly Bakongo soldiers with perhaps some stiffening of Hausas. The Force grew to eight companies and 2,000 men, and saw its first fighting against Arab slavers who penetrated from East Africa nearly to Stanleyville. Then in the nineties also there were engagements against the Sudan Mahdists, when King Léopold took over the Lado enclave in the south-east Sudan (only finally restored to the Sudan in 1910). Three mutinies occurred also in the nineties, in each case inspired by Arab half-breeds who had been press-ganged into the Force.

In the First World War the Force Publique fought against the Germans in East Africa and Rhodesia, and also alongside British and French troops in the Cameroons. In the Second World War, four Congolese battalions played a distinguished part in the Abyssinian campaign: at the end, after a hard day's fighting at Saio on 3 July 1941, nine generals, 370 officers, 2,500 Italians, and 1,500 Askaris surrendered to the small Congolese force, followed by the 11,000 troops remaining south of the Blue Nile. In 1942 a hospital unit served in Somalia and Madagascar, and a brigade in Nigeria. This force was later sent to Egypt where it carried out guard duties in the Delta. It returned to the Congo in 1944, in which year also a Congolese Field Hospital went to the India/Burma front. Lundula, who was to be the first Congolese Commander-in-Chief, had been a sergeant in this unit.

After the war the Force Publique reverted to its dual role of internal security force with one company in each administrative district, and infantry battalions divided into three commands with, in addition, an independent mobile brigade. By 1960 the whole Force totalled some 25,000, with 1,000 Belgian officers and warrant officers.

When Independence came, at breakneck speed, loose ends abounded and people simply hoped against hope that the gamble might come off. I had proposed, more than once in the weeks before, that Hammarskjøld and Eugene Black should be invited from the U.N.O. and from the World Bank to be present in Leopoldville at the date of Independence, not only for the steadying effect which their presence might have but so that they could be available for advice, consultation, and possible offers of assistance. In the event, Ralph Bunche did call at Léopoldville on his way back from a trip elsewhere in Africa (I do not know whether this had anything to do with my suggestions). Nobly as he strove when the storm broke, this was not quite the same thing. He was to become the first head of U.N. operations in the Congo; but he was unsuited by training and temperament for this and his health gave way by the end of August when he left the Congo.

If Lumumba had been a different kind of person, if there had not been a mutiny in the army, and if virtually all the Belgian officers had not then left, just conceivably a Congolese government could have established itself throughout the country in a peaceful succession. But this was not to be; and I do not think the chances were improved—as far as the army holding together was concerned—by a tour of all units which its Belgian Commander-in-Chief made in the weeks before Independence. His theme throughout was that the Congo depended on the Army, that life would be harder for the soldiers after Independence than before, and that in fact Independence would mean for them no change or only a change for the worse. When the troops saw that indeed no magic change occurred on Independence and that while civilian Congolese replaced Belgians in the seats of power no army sergeant became even a 2nd Lieutenant, the balloon went up. The fragile unity which an all-Congolese army showed, in the face of very diverse tribal groupings and virtually no feeling of Congolese nationality, was shattered overnight in early July. But this is to anticipate.

The great day of Independence arrived. King Baudouin, accompanied by Ministers, came from Belgium to Léopoldville for the formal hand-over. The ceremony was arranged in the splendid new building, reminiscent of a Presidency Government House in India, which had been constructed as a residence for the Governor-General but had been quickly and acceptably transformed in its latest stages into a parliament house. It is indicative of the Belgian approach to the whole question of Congolese independence that as late as 1959 this great mansion was being constructed with a view to gubernatorial occupation for, obviously, twenty-five or fifty years more.

Here on the morning of 30 June came the King of Belgium and delegates from all over the world to witness the birth of this newest of the African states. It was a beautiful morning in the middle of the Congo's cool weather, and we walked (Lord Dundee had come as the special

British representative) the few hundred yards to this new Palais de la Nation, as it was now to be called, joining there in the throng of press, delegates, and invited guests. It was with very different and uneasy feelings that the company came away some three or four hours later.

The great rotunda was filled with members of both houses of the legislature, special representatives of most of the countries of the world (including all British territories in Africa except the Gambia and the Federation of Rhodesia and Nyasaland), leading members of the administration and notabilities of the Congo, a numerous Belgian delegation which included the Prime Minister and other Ministers, and as many of the public as succeeded in making their way into the building. When everyone was in place, King Baudouin and President Kasavubu entered together and took their seats to one side, below the dais on which sat the two Speakers of the Assembly and Senate.

The King made the first speech, devoted mainly to an account of what Belgium had done in the Congo and including also advice—sensible, if perhaps out of place on this occasion—on how the Congo should manage its affairs in the future. The King claimed that the movement towards independence all over Africa had found the greatest understanding among the Belgians: a curious way of describing the handling by Belgium of Congo events in recent months. He also cited, as one of the two greatest dangers facing the Congo, the 'attraction exercised over certain regions by foreign powers ready to take advantage of the least weakness'. Considering that the neighbours of the Congo were effectively at that time Britain, France, and Portugal, who are among Belgium's closest allies, this seemed to me a most unfortunate statement. It surely ill became the King of the Belgians to beat the drum of suspicion of foreign aggression in order to try and create unity in the Congo. So far as I know, this statement by him was in no way justified by the facts (the stationing of troops on the Rhodesian and Angolan borders was a local precaution of those territories to deal with possible refugees).

The King was followed by President Kasavubu, whose speech was sensible, moderate, and flavoured with a certain humility. Much of it was taken up with the need to foster national unity in a country of such great size and complexity. He spoke appreciatively, too, of the benefits which Western civilization had brought: a common language as the vehicle of communication, a legal system which had influenced the evolution of native custom, and, above all, the benign effects of Christian teaching and European culture on the peoples of the Congo. For the time being, this speech ruled out any possibility of a separate Bakongo state.

The third speech was by Prime Minister Lumumba—hard, bitter, accusatory, and xenophobic, directed against the Belgians. 'We have known the contempt, the insults, the blows which we have had to suffer morning, noon, and night because we were niggers. Who can forget that *"tu"* was used to a black man and *"vous"* reserved for the whites?' 'We have seen that there was one law for the whites and another for the blacks.' There were many other such phrases, so that at one point my neighbour, a Belgian, was moved to say to me that he thought the King would rise and leave the ceremony. The King did indeed lean across to President Kasavubu in the middle of Lumumba's speech and ask whether he had known of its contents in advance. The reply was negative; had it been otherwise it is possible that the King would have left. It was remarked by many that in the course of the King's speech Lumumba had been seen furiously making notes on the script for his own speech. Perhaps the King praised the work of Belgium too much, although there was much for Belgium to be proud of. At all events the effect of Lumumba's speech on all the Belgians present was profound and humiliating. The day was difficult in any case for them to live through, with no sense of satisfaction of a job well done in bringing the Congo to independence; this was an additional trial. The official lunch which followed the ceremony was delayed for two hours while the King and Belgian Cabinet Ministers considered whether to boycott it and return at once to Brussels. In the end, a compromise was reached whereby they attended the lunch and Lumumba proposed a brief toast to the King and to the Belgians which was almost fulsome in its terms, but which years afterwards still leaves an impression of insincerity. This could not efface the memory of the morning speech, and it will be long before the Belgians who were present will be able to remember the occasion without anger.

I am not sure what moved Lumumba to make such a bitter speech. It had not been cleared by his colleagues, and indeed up to the last minute there had been no provision in the programme for a speech by him at all. He told Lord Dundee and myself, when we called on him the next day, that he had had to make that speech in order to satisfy the people—so that they might get out of their system, so to speak, their feelings about the Belgians. No doubt, also, he was using this occasion to put himself on the Pan-African anti-imperialist map and trying to create the necessary myth of epic struggle. I believe, however, that he was partly actuated by the Belgian intrigues and manoeuvres against him in recent weeks, when they had tried their hardest to prevent him from becoming Prime Minister. He knew all about this and was justly incensed. He must have resented, too, the King's paternal advice on how to manage Congo affairs. Even so, the ceremony of 30 June was not a seemly occasion for such an outburst, which spoiled an otherwise splendid occasion. We all had a cold and disorganized lunch and returned finally home to try and work out what this inauspicious event portended.

In a further effort to overtake the harm which was done by his speech, Lumumba made a special broadcast to Belgium the next day. He appealed to young Belgians to come out and make a career in the Congo and assured Belgians of the gratitude which the Congo felt for all they had done. He asked investors to help develop the great resources of the Congo, and not to misunderstand his government's policy towards foreign capital: 'we shall protect investments which truly help the increase of national production just as much as we fight against unjustified positions of privilege.' He and his government wished 'that Belgium should be the first country to take the outstretched hand of friendship of the Congo'. It was too late, however. Lumumba had revealed himself; and although his words at Independence did not of themselves determine the Congo's subsequent relations with Belgium, they clearly made more difficult hopes of friendly understanding between the two countries.

Four days of holiday marked Independence, a long week-end of mingled hopes and fears. Would the Congo dissolve into anarchy because 'men of intemperate minds cannot be free'? Would 'their passions forge their fetters'? No one could be sure. *'Nous nous trouvons'*, as a senior Belgian official remarked to me, *'devant l'inconnu complet.'*

Official lunches and dinners, processions, games, folk dancing, and fireworks—two full days were taken up with this programme, about which the only significant point is that they all took place without incident and in many cases in an atmosphere of genuine and friendly popular rejoicing. There were no attacks on Europeans; no murders, rapes, arson, and so on, which had been the nightmare of Belgians for months past, and the thought of which had already sent tens of thousands of them back to Belgium. There were, during the four days of holiday, a number of minor brawls in some of the African communes, serious enough to justify an appeal for calm over the radio by the Prime Minister and a statement by him that all necessary steps would be taken to restore order. A certain amount of this had been expected, as the Independence celebrations came at the end of the month and carried with them an additional payment for Congolese workers. An enormous consumption of beer had taken place. This, added to the disgruntlement which was still felt by supporters of Bolikango, a leader from the Équateur province who was much respected but considered to be too much in with the Belgians (and partly for this reason had been defeated by Kasavubu for the Presidency), was enough to cause such disturbances as took place. Apart from Kasai, where Lulua and Baluba tribesmen again came to blows near Luluabourg, there was no news from anywhere in the Congo of disorderly behaviour; even from Stanleyville where, on 29 June, an excited planter shot at his chauffeur, missed him, but killed an African woman coming out of a shop.

Only the soldiers had had no holiday. On the contrary, they had been hard at work in aid of the police all these four days; and that followed weeks and months of tension in the Kasai tribal fights and the enforcement of curfews. By 5 July things began to slide. General Janssens, himself for long under considerable strain, had a serious difference of opinion with Lumumba over matters of army organization, and showed himself unbending in the new political situation which Independence had created. This attitude, and the implication that nothing at all had changed for them, annoyed and alarmed the Congolese troops, and a confused day followed with some excitement in the army camp in the capital. Elsewhere in Léopoldville things went normally on, and by evening, thanks to Lumumba's personal intervention, a superficial calm had returned to the camp. By then, however, a similar but more serious situation was developing at Thysville, a garrison town some ninety miles to the west of Léopoldville. The troops there refused to obey their officers and took over the armoury.

On 6 July some of the Congolese Army in Léopoldville refused to accept the orders of their officers—particularly some Flemish officers; and Janssens tendered his resignation to Lumumba because he was not allowed to deal with this threat in the way which he considered necessary, by using Belgian troops from the two Belgian bases to suppress the meeting. Some quick comings and goings around the Prime Minister's residence (of which we were practically neighbours) and the Palais de la Nation marked the afternoon of that day. The next morning was quiet except for a variety of rumours, involving also stories of some police indiscipline and wild behaviour by Congolese soldiers in Thysville and the neighbouring region. A drastic reorganization of the army was decreed by Lumumba, and ex-Sergeant-Major Lundula was appointed Commander-in-Chief. All officer posts were Africanized and all ranks promoted. Mobutu was made Chief of Staff with the rank of Colonel: he had spent nine years in the army, becoming a warrant officer by the time of his departure to become a journalist in 1956, at the age of twenty-seven. Lundula, who belonged to a small tribe allied to Lumumba's, was at this time working as a local government official in a small town in Katanga; it was many days before he could reach Léopoldville.

We went to bed as usual about eleven o'clock on 7 July, only to receive a telephone call soon afterwards asking if anything was known of a revolt in the Congolese Army. For the next half-hour an unusual number of cars passed our house, in front and behind, since it lay between the road along the river front and a parallel road behind, which ran through a residential area. The telephone rang a couple more times with similar inquiries, and then the first British subject appeared on the doorstep to know what was going on. Rapidly increasing motor traffic and sporadic telephone calls made it clear that something serious was amiss, and that we might as well get up again. For several hours through the night this went on—more calls, more traffic, more visitors; and we reached 5 o'clock in the morning with some thirty people in our house, endless cups of tea being brewed, and a general state of mounting uneasiness and complicating information. The ferry service maintained by small steamers across the river between Léopoldville and Brazzaville did not work at nights; but now from our house, from about 1.30 a.m., we could see the big river steamers, which normally went the 1,100 miles up river to Stanleyville, plying back and forth across to Brazzaville, and the Brazzaville docks were all lit up on the other side. Gradually the story pieced itself together.

On the previous day there had been an outright army mutiny at Thysville, and some wives of Belgian officers there had been raped. All, I believe, but one of the Belgians who could do so then left incontinently for Léopoldville, by rail and by road convoy. These people arrived in the evening at Léopoldville and panic spread like a bush fire among their colleagues and a widening circle of Belgian residents, particularly after the train bringing a number of injured reached Léopoldville soon after 9 o'clock. Details of what had happened did not come to Léopoldville during the day because the mutineers had control of the army communications. The cars which we had heard passing our house had been taking their occupants to the ferry point to go across to Brazzaville; with the result that by morning, for a quarter of a mile around the ferry departure jetty, there was a solid block of abandoned cars. The big river steamers had been started up by Belgian engineers and used to ferry the fleeing crowds across the river. The Congolese Army became very excited by the massing, as it seemed to them, of the Belgians at this central point in the city, and interpreted it as being a regrouping to win the city back for Belgium. Little did they know that the exact opposite was the case, and that the one idea in the minds of all the Belgians was to get out of the country as soon as possible. But while this mutual panic built up on both sides, jeep-loads of Congolese soldiery roamed the streets, a tommy-gun in the hand of each man and his finger on the trigger; among other activities, they stopped isolated cars to search for arms. In the group of people who had come to our house during the night was a South African couple. It became clear by the early morning that there was no point in their staying on in Léopoldville at this time, and I agreed that they could well move across the river. The two of them went off to collect some clothes from their house, less than half a mile from us; but they were back within minutes, the wife scarlet in the face and both very angry. They had been stopped by a Congolese Army patrol and searched for arms, in the course of which a Congolese soldier had put his hand down her dress to feel for a revolver, this being known as the place where those Belgian women who were armed often kept the weapon. Perhaps she had never in her life even shaken hands with a black man; but that episode so affronted her as to leave her almost incoherent. However, they set out again, this time successfully, collected some clothes, and crossed the river.

From the scattered pieces of information which had reached me by 6 o'clock in the morning, it was obvious that a decision was urgently required as to whether or not British subjects should be advised to leave. I came to the conclusion that it would be well for women and children to go across the river to Brazzaville until the situation became clearer, and that any men who had no particular need to stay should also depart; though I did not think that there was risk of physical danger for British subjects. My own wife was very reluctant to go, but as it was impossible for me to advise others to do what I did not do myself, she also left with the group from our house. So did many of those whom we could contact by telephone with the same advice. They all reached, without serious mishap, the departure point of the ferry and crossed to Brazzaville, where the suddenly improvised reception arrangements and the kindness and efficiency of local residents and the Brazzaville authorities were admirable. My wife returned two days later and was followed some days afterwards by a few other wives. Some, however, did not return for six months.

Mounting confusion in Léopoldville, to which the massive departure of so many Belgians contributed (it was a case of 'the day the dam broke') made it impossible to know how events would turn out. The panic reaction of the Belgians made things steadily worse and produced scenes which brought shame to some of the Belgians still remaining. During that first 'night of terror', as the British press had it, houses were abandoned—some with dogs locked inside, some with lights on or windows open—in the mad scramble to seek safety in numbers, near the Belgian Embassy and the dock area whence lay the way to safety and freedom across the river. Fear bred fear, and the Congolese apprehension that the Belgians were grouping to attack them resulted in bands of soldiers, mutinous or otherwise—the distinction was not clear for several days—roaming the streets and stopping cars and persons, men and women, roughly and crudely. They recovered a good many weapons, the owners of which were usually taken away to spend an hour or two (unharmed) in a military camp, until the intervention of a Congolese Minister or other person of authority secured their release.

The fear and panic which had gripped the minds of many was naturally increased when news arrived in due course of similar breakdowns in provincial capitals like Luluabourg and Stanleyville; for the army mutiny which had begun in Thysville rolled over the whole Congo like a tidal wave in the next few days. The stories were often exaggerated but sometimes, unfortunately, not; and for an uncomfortable period the Europeans in Luluabourg were imprisoned in a central building in which they had assembled and which the local Congolese troops started to mortar when they would not surrender. At Stanleyville there was a relatively peaceful transfer from Belgian officers to self-appointed Congolese successors. That did not prevent, however, the credulous from spreading rumours. The Congo river divides Stanleyville (now named Kisangani), and at 11.30 p.m. one night a message reached the Belgian Club that all Europeans on the other side of the river had been massacred and that everyone must flee. An Englishman who happened to be sitting there with a Belgian told me later that in a flash the clientele got up and departed, leaving him and his friend to finish their beer alone. That done, he rang up an acquaintance on the other side of the river, who gruffly answered the telephone, obviously having been aroused from sleep. In reply to the inane question 'Are you still alive?' the reply came back, 'What the hell do you mean?' My informant then explained that he had been told that everyone had been murdered on the other side of the river; he was informed, in reply, that nothing at all had happened, and was told in colourful language what he could do with himself.

The rolling revolution passed on to Élisabethville in another day or two, the Belgian exodus from that city being led, so I was later informed, by the local chief of police. Very serious consequences might have ensued there had not one Belgian officer remained behind to defend the armoury with a handful of Congolese troops prepared to obey him. As a result, only four Europeans, including the Italian Vice-Consul, were killed in Élisabethville on that Saturday, 9 July. Belgian paratroopers arrived from Kamina base at 6 a.m. on the Sunday and rapidly took over control. The mutineers mostly fled, not, however, before a number of them were killed—exactly how many will never be known but it was certainly a larger number than the Europeans killed the day before. Most of the many hundreds of Belgians who fled into Northern Rhodesia returned a few days later.

During this time all army command posts held by Belgians in the Force Publique, now renamed the Congolese Army, were handed over to Congolese. The highest rank which any Congolese had hitherto held was sergeant-major and the new officer corps had therefore to be selected from the body of N.C.O.s and ex-N.C.O.s which included Lundula and also Mobutu (who was at that time a newly-appointed Secretary of State for Defence in Lumumba's Cabinet). The appointments were made, sometimes by a sort of soviet election, at other centres by direct nomination, and were quickly completed.

Kasavubu and Lumumba set out on a rapid tour round the Congo (but leaving out Katanga) to make or confirm, as the case might be, their appointments. Only a handful of Belgian officers remained at their posts out of 1,000, of whom perhaps 750 had been in the Congo at the time of Independence. None of these, however, retained command of troops; they stayed as advisers or experts. It was not known whether the troops would obey their new officers; nor, therefore, whether the army might not rapidly disintegrate into warring tribal factions. The general jumpiness everywhere, the reaction of fear and panic by many of the Congolese troops, and increasing doubt as to the capacity of Lumumba's government to deal with this kind of situation gave a sharp edge to daily life. And yet the very momentum of the machine had a certain stabilizing effect.

Some of the newly promoted officers made good; some did not. The inexperience of the central command made things more difficult; but very gradually a certain control spread, beginning in Léopoldville itself. It never covered the whole country in my time in the Congo. Orientale province, particularly when Antoine Gizenga in due course set up his rump Lumumbist Ministry in Stanleyville and was joined there by Lundula, remained mostly outside any control from the capital. And Katanga presented a different but equally serious problem, of which more will be said.

The revolt in the Force Publique was something which no one had foreseen, although with the advantage of hindsight it may be said that it should have been realized that the Congolese troops had been too far tested by action in support of the civil power for many weeks previously, and at the same time had received no visible proof that Independence was to make any change at all in their conditions. In the light of what happened later there would seem to have been latent in the Force Publique sufficient causes for this mutiny. The uprising was at no point directed against foreigners as such—it was for the ending of a colonial system and against the Belgian officers who continued to embody that régime for them. It later became known that Africans who had reported, to their officers, the mutterings inside the Force Publique, had been severely punished instead of having their grievances and ambitions sympathetically considered. In some places, the brutal and licentious soldiery ran wild, and deplorable incidents occurred—the beating of men and the raping of women. These episodes, however, were not many, seen in the context of the vast size of the Congo and the many scattered European communities which existed all over it. They were enough, however, to cause fear and consternation everywhere, and gave an unwelcome touch of danger to ordinary daily life.

It has been argued that communist propaganda was behind the mutiny and expulsion of the Belgians. I was sceptical of this at the time and have since remained so. No doubt there were communist efforts, including those made by the Belgian Communist Party itself, to prevent the development of normal relations with the West. These were also made by the Czechs, the staff of whose Consulate the Russians used as their 'running dogs'—to use their own terminology—and agents for passing money to Congolese politicians, selecting and sending young Congolese for training in communist countries, and so on. All this was well known at the time. But I am convinced that Lumumba was not a communist—apart from anything else, he had not the serious or dedicated beliefs even to be that. And if the Belgian Communist Party gave him money, so did big business in Belgium, a fact also well known at the time. He of course was prepared to take money from any source. There is no need to postulate elaborate and successful communist plots for what happened in the Congo. I am not one of those who have been impressed, in my five years in the Middle East followed by five years in Africa, with communist and particularly Russian skill in diplomacy. It is not necessary to assume this to account for what happened; and, after all, there is not one country in Africa or the Middle East with a communist government despite the expenditure of vast sums and much effort by the communist powers. Many of these countries, it is true, have adopted forms of government similar to those which exist in communist countries. But presumably even the communists would not claim that they had invented the idea of dictatorship, for example, or one-party rule. There is no need, therefore, to credit communist powers with victories they did not win.

Deeper, perhaps, and unexpressed was the feeling that the Belgians were still there and would not go away; that they insisted on clinging to the Congo. Not only were all Belgian officers and most officials still in their places immediately after Independence, but Belgian flags were left up in the streets for days after 30 June (where they were not unofficially taken down and sometimes torn up); the Belgian Ambassador issued a prim little announcement that he was to be known not as Belgian Ambassador but as something more: 'Head of the Belgian Diplomatic Mission'; and so on.

In the event, the wrath—and fear—of the Congolese was for the Belgians and more particularly for the Flemish among them. It was a pleasure and a safeguard during the following weeks to be British; and on many occasions a statement that this was so completely changed a hostile crowd into a friendly one. Not always, of course, because illiterate soldiery did not always recognize the difference. Whereas some 20,000 Belgians fled, comparatively few United Kingdom British felt the need to leave the country, although most sent their families away. Even Cypriots found the benefits of a British passport; but several hundred did in fact leave, many of them from the small towns of Orientale province near the Sudan and Uganda borders.

6

Then began a curious existence in Léopoldville: a great city where civil and military authority had broken down and no one knew from hour to hour or day to day what might happen. Life, in some important respects, went on normally: water and electricity supplies never failed and the dust-carts came round punctually; some food shops and markets remained open; the post office was intermittently open, although the long-distance telephone service hardly functioned at all. The chief evidence of life in the streets was the continued stream of Belgians heading for the port and safety. The same pattern of mutiny or disorderly hand-over repeated itself first in the police force in Léopoldville and then all over the Congo. From the remoter parts of the country the refugees made for neighbouring territories; from the interior of the Congo, planeloads soon began to reach Léopoldville airport, which sometimes was closed by the Congolese Army and sometimes opened again, depending upon the whim of whichever group of mutinous soldiers was in evidence at a particular time and place. The same intermittent freedom of movement existed at the ferry port of Léopoldville, so that one was continually dealing on an hour-to-hour basis with individual problems.

A strange episode on the first night of the troubles was the rumour that a party of Russians were arriving at the airport; my query as to whether they had snow on their boots was not understood by my informant. This led the mutinous Force Publique to organize a party to repel them, not out of any anti-communist feeling but because they believed that Russian officers were coming to replace their Belgian officers; and they did not want any but Congolese officers over them. This story, it later became clear, had been put about by disgruntled anti-Lumumba politicians, in the hope of discrediting the Prime Minister by proving that he really was a communist who was preparing in this way for a communist coup d'état. The affair had its bizarre side, because there was in fact a large Russian aircraft at the airport which had brought the Russian delegation to the Independence celebrations and had waited to take them on a projected tour of the Congo. The crew of this aircraft were kept under arrest for some time by the Congolese troops; and my Czech colleague telephoned to me in the early hours to ask what he should do about the plane, and also whether I thought that his special ambassador who had come for the celebrations would be safe in the house which had been allotted to him.

Several Congolese Ministers (notably, perhaps, Justin Bomboko, the Foreign Minister) showed up extremely well during those difficult and dangerous days. They were tireless in their efforts to iron out differences between groups of Europeans and members of the Force Publique, and succeeded often in preventing ugly incidents. For four vital days the Head of State and Prime Minister were absent from the capital. They were engaged in the same process as they had fairly successfully carried through in Léopoldville—nominating Congolese officers to posts of command in the army and police in all the provincial capitals. For the junior officers, they sometimes adopted the expedient of asking the men to make an election. Kasavubu and Lumumba were, however, not allowed by their Belgian pilot (acting on Belgian orders) to travel as and when they wished, because the Belgians did not want them back in Léopoldville at that moment. During their absence, M. Bomboko and M. Delvaux, the Congo Minister-Designate in Brussels, took the initiative (allegedly prompted by my American colleague) of inviting the United States of America to send three thousand troops into Léopoldville province to restore order. This decision was repudiated by the Prime Minister and the Head of State on their return to Léopoldville and nearly resulted in the dismissal of the two Ministers most concerned. It would not have been the right answer.

After the first four or five days of extreme confusion and variable danger, followed by the news of similar events all over the country, Léopoldville again set the fashion for a second wave of disorder by the outbreak of strikes in all the large industrial and business enterprises. These were in support of demands for special awards to celebrate Independence and sometimes also for the Africanization of the senior posts. Most firms gave way at once on the money claims, but others held out and some of the largest, for example, OTRACO, the state-owned transport organization, had some days of very difficult negotiations. These strikes, however, were all soon settled in the capital, if not elsewhere; but nothing like full working could resume because nearly all the Belgian overseers and officials had left. This had serious effects on transport and employment.

The Head of State and Prime Minister countered the Cabinet request for U.S. aid by a supposedly joint message to Khrushchev about possible Russian aid, though in fact the message was sent by Lumumba without the knowledge of Kasavubu. Notwithstanding, on 11 July Lumumba appealed to the U.N. for assistance in restoring order in the Congolese Army, and the decision of the Security Council on 14 July overtook the proposal to Russia. This Resolution was in the following terms:

The Security Council, considering the report of the Secretary-General on a request for United Nations action in relation to the Republic of the Congo,
Considering the request for military assistance addressed to the Secretary-General by the President and the Prime Minister of the Republic of the Congo (S/4382),
1. Calls upon the Government of Belgium to withdraw its troops from the territory of the Republic of the Congo;
2. Decides to authorize the Secretary-General to take the necessary steps, in consultation with the Government of the Republic of the Congo, to provide the Government with such military assistance as may be necessary until, through the efforts of the Congolese Government with the technical assistance of the United Nations, the national security forces may be able, in the opinion of the Government, to meet fully their tasks;
3. Requests the Secretary-General to report to the Security Council as appropriate.

It is important, for the understanding of subsequent events, to note particularly (1) that the U.N. military involvement in the Congo was at the request of the Congolese and intended to supply such help as the Congolese wanted and needed (their opinion being impliedly decisive in this) to put their country on its feet; and (2) the Security Council's prime requirement of the removal of Belgian troops. These were (by arrangement with the Congolese, reached before Independence) at two bases which had not been evacuated. The Congolese, by the date of the Security Council Resolution, feared that these troops, at Kamina in the south-east and Kitona on the coast, might be used in an attempt to 'recapture' the Congo and take away its independence. There was no justification for such a fear. Belgium used the troops (not perhaps always wisely or well) to protect its own citizens: it would have been indefensible for the Belgian government not to have done so in cases of dire necessity. But this gave grounds for the allegations against them, both in the Congo and in New York. And these allegations found further justification in the support which some Belgians and Belgian companies gave to Moïse Tshombe in his separatist bid for the independence of Katanga. For a variety of reasons, therefore, a profound distrust of Belgium and all things Belgian was implanted in the U.N.

The first Security Council Resolution was quickly followed by others adopted on 22 July, 9 August, and 20 September. These were passed to keep pace with the rapidly evolving situation in the Congo; the first two of them were specifically based on reports and recommendations of Dag Hammarskjøld, the Secretary-General. They repeated the call to Belgium to withdraw its troops; and all three enjoined the Secretary-General to continue 'vigorous action' to 'assist the central government of the Congo in the restoration and maintenance of law and order'. The full texts of these and later U.N. Resolutions on the Congo are readily available in U.N. publications. Here I only wish to draw attention to the fact that, inevitably, much in this great operation turned on the personality of the Secretary-General. Hammarskjøld was a man of patent integrity and ability. He had, however, much of the Swedish characteristics of clinical detachment and devotion to abstract ideas, as well as a certain reserve, which affected, in my opinion, both his understanding of people and his ability to take them with him in his thinking. He saw the Congo operation—as indeed it was—as a growth-point for the U.N. into a vast new area. His own subtle mind used this opportunity to further the ideals which he cherished of building up the power and the authority of the U.N. and its Secretary-General.

By voting for the Resolution of 14 July, as well as the next two, Russia of course became fully associated with the U.N. action in the Congo, along with the other members of the Security Council. Troops from some African countries were already in the Congo without having waited for the first Security Council Resolution; and the announcement by Hammarskjøld that three European countries would also contribute troops helped, although only slightly, to calm the fears of the Belgians at the influx of African troops to the country. As already mentioned, under the Treaty of Friendship between the Congo and Belgium, signed on 29 June, Belgium had retained the temporary use of two bases in the Congo, to enable orderly withdrawal to be completed. The mutiny in the Congolese Army and breakdown of law and order in many places led the Belgian government to bring in additional troops to safeguard the lives of their nationals; and as part of that operation the Belgian troops took over the city of Léopoldville. The immediate Congolese reaction to all this was to demand the rupture of diplomatic relations with Belgium, the denunciation of the Treaty of 29 June with Belgium, and the withdrawal of all Belgian troops from the Congo; they also demanded help from the U.N. to expel the Belgian troops.

There were major political problems to be resolved concerning the relationship of the U.N. troops to the Congolese government, and the authority of the U.N. troops to act, in case of need, for the maintenance of law and order, independently of the wishes of that government. This was a problem which was never satisfactorily solved. It soon began to look as if Lumumba had accepted that the U.N. troops remained under U.N. command solely and that they had come at his government's invitation (although not to do his government's bidding)—both points which he seemed at first to contest. U.N. technical aid was also promised and food began to arrive. If the general countrywide transport organization could resume more normal functioning in the near future, there would be no serious food problem except perhaps so far as concerned the unemployed in the cities.

Under Ralph Bunche's overall direction, von Horn took command of the U.N. military forces and Sture Linner of the technical assistance programme. Both sides of the U.N.'s operations grew rapidly, and inevitably the need for constant improvisation amid chaotic working conditions made it impossible at first to work out any long-term plans. All the U.N.'s problems were accentuated by Lumumba's temperamental behaviour and the confusion with which he was faced in the administration and economic (not to speak of the political) life of the country. At the same time, the whole world came to the Congo, and Lumumba had to adapt himself to dealing with representatives of many countries. There were those with long-standing interests in the Congo, notably Belgium itself; and others for which this newly independent country seemed an admirable point of entry into central Africa, with rewards of many kinds to be collected.

This, then, was the first of what might be distinguished as the three main themes that were to act and react on each other continuously during the remaining twelve months that I spent in the Congo—the impact of the United Nations and outside countries on what had hitherto been a closed world existing in isolation on its own. The second was the struggle for political power among the Congolese leaders themselves, pursued sometimes with frenzied irresponsibility and ruthless brutality. The third was Katanga, about which perhaps something should be said at this point.

Katanga was a special province of the Congo, and Tshombe an unusual politician. The province contains extremely rich mineral deposits, of which copper is only the best known. At the time of Independence the copper-mining company employed some 2,000 Belgians in Katanga and 600 back in Belgium. As copper was being produced at the time for less than £100 per ton and sold on the world market at £250 per ton, the profits on an annual production of nearly 300,000 tons were obviously large, even allowing for all transport and marketing expenses. The results of the May elections produced at first an impasse in Katanga. Tshombe's party obtained 25 seats in the Provincial Assembly out of a total of 60, while his principal rival, Jason Sendwe, obtained 22. Sendwe promptly stated that he would not accept the result of the elections and his group staged a walk-out from the first meeting of the Assembly. This meeting had been called to select additional members as required by the constitution to be co-opted by the elected members; but a clause in the constitution laid down that at least two-thirds of the membership should take part in the co-opting procedure and this was manifestly impossible after the withdrawal of Sendwe's contingent. A Belgian threat to alter the law induced Sendwe to bring his group back into a subsequent meeting, muttering threats, however, of setting up a separate state in North Katanga, where Sendwe and his supporters came from. The prescribed procedure was followed, however, and a provincial government took office with Tshombe as Prime Minister.

Tshombe had been disappointed, on the formation of the central government, at not receiving the share in it to which he considered that his party was entitled. He had claimed certain important portfolios, including Finance, which Lumumba had been unwilling to concede. Before agreement could be reached the mutiny in the Army broke out. Tshombe had by then been waiting in Léopoldville for some days and decided to return to Katanga, preferring to consolidate his local position there. In the mounting confusion of the succeeding days he thought that he saw his chance to cut loose from the centre. Élisabethville, the capital of Katanga, went through its convulsive mutiny in early July (when a tidal wave of Belgians left for Northern Rhodesia) but emerged from it relatively intact (and the tidal wave flowed back). The end of that month saw Tshombe securely in power and the province well under control. The Belgian presence remained as before, and Tshombe continued to employ many Belgian officials in the administration. By early August no U.N. troops had reached Katanga and none were either needed or wanted by Tshombe. Von Horn gives a graphic description of his attempt to persuade the U.N. to leave well alone in Katanga and to concentrate its effort where it was needed. He was overborne however and Hammarskjøld succeeded later against strong protests by Tshombe in getting a U.N. military contingent into Katanga. Lumumba refused to accept that Tshombe should be left alone in his glory, making declarations about Katanga secession from time to time. The separatist movement in Katanga obsessed Lumumba: everything he did in late August was conditioned by his desire to crush and humiliate Tshombe. In this Lumumba had the full backing of the Afro-Asian group and he launched his disastrous military attack towards Katanga when the U.N. refused to help him. When this failed, Tshombe made it clear that he would not deal with any Congo government which included Lumumba. There is no doubt that Tshombe enjoyed the support of the Belgians in his refusal to subject himself to Léopoldville. In this he was carrying on a tradition of hostility (as Belgian officials had long before explained to me) between Katanga and the centre. Katanga had always felt that the province was being used as a milch cow for the whole Congo, and there was a latent nationalist feeling about this on which Tshombe could build. That the Belgian government ever went so far as to counsel seccession to Tshombe I do not believe. But I have no doubt that many individual Belgians and perhaps Belgian companies did so, and that Tshombe had been strongly tempted to try it on. Encouragement to him came too from Rhodesia. It was only long after I had left the Congo that I learnt the reason for a sudden cooling-off in my relations with the Belgian representatives at one point—it was because they believed that the British government was behind what was a purely Rhodesian initiative of which, of course, I knew nothing at the time. This would seem, however, to confirm the correctness of the Belgian government's attitude towards Tshombe's ideas of secession. Not one country in the world (including Belgium) was prepared to recognize a separate state of Katanga, and Tshombe in the end was forced to accept that. For many months he caused worldwide repercussions by a demand for independence—this I believe was a political ploy once he knew, as he did after the first couple of months, that he could never succeed in a bid for complete independence. He tried for long to get greater autonomy for Katanga, but in the end he failed here too.

Yet Tshombe was greatly misjudged at this time and violently condemned. Without going into the rights and wrongs of Katanga separatism, or the desirability of the attempt to bring it about, it needs to be said of Tshombe that, in wanting to separate from the rest of the Congo, he wanted no more than, for example, one of the areas of Nigeria has been fighting for, with the support of some African, and other countries. The keeping together of fortuitous colonial groupings is bound to cause tension. For years more than one African country has encouraged the separatist movement in Eritrea; and the U.N. itself separated the unfortunate Ruanda-Urundi into two halves. No one in the U.N. ever mentions those things, let alone becomes wildly excited about them. True, this was not the best time to discuss separatism in the Congo, with generalized confusion everywhere. At the emergency session on 30 September, the U.N. had officially endorsed the territorial integrity of the Congo and could properly point that out. But why was Tshombe's crime so heinous as to arouse such fury in the U.N. and in so many countries of the world? I believe that the explanation was simply that Tshombe was an extrovert who got on too easily with people, including white people, and could use Belgian officials with no sense of inferiority. He had been a businessman for years, at times prosperous. A Belgian in Élisabethville told me that when Tshombe had bought his first truck before the War, the word had gone round the town like wildfire, 'A black man has bought a truck.' Tshombe could thereafter go into a bank or office in Élisabethville and be received as an honoured visitor, sat down, and given a cup of coffee. Tshombe certainly in my opinion used Belgians in the months of his power in Katanga more than they used him. But that an African could be openly friendly with Europeans and mix easily with them was at that time anathema to many in Africa; he seemed to lack any racialist feeling. All this made him suspect to the U.N. as did the praise lavished on him by the Belgians; and as did to some extent the fact that his father-in-law was a great tribal chief. Secondly, to give dispassionate consideration to the possibility that even the largest country in Africa could shed part of itself would have involved many others in giving thought to the redrawing of their own boundaries. Although the British and others had earlier been criticized for creating artificial boundaries in Africa, no African government which inherited power in such an artificially created unity showed any inclination to achieve more homogeneous groupings. So for these two reasons Tshombe had to be subdued.

Lumumba failed to do so by force in early August; a meeting in the Congo of representatives of African states at the end of August failed by persuasion; and so later did the U.N. Conciliation Commission which came to the Congo in late November and spent many weeks in the country. But this is to anticipate. While Katanga contributed its *obbligato* in the background, rising to the short intensity of the attack on it through Kasai province in August, another theme was playing itself out in the capital. By mid-July serious strains had been produced within the Cabinet. So preoccupied had all Ministers been with the immediate situation from day to day that they rarely met to discuss policy. No programme had been presented to the legislature by the government; and Lumumba's habit of arrogating to himself the right to speak in the name of the government without consulting his colleagues was being increasingly resented. 'The crisis', I wrote on 18 July, 'will have to go on yet further, I fear, before any chance of Lumumba's being evicted from the Premiership would become practical politics.' Nor was the general situation helped by a series of virulently anti-foreign speeches by Anicet Kashamura, the Minister of Information, who unfortunately controlled the radio network.

The effect of these events upon the future of the Congo was impossible to determine. Obviously a major setback had been suffered by the new state, complicated by the apparent determination of Katanga province to secede. The skill shown by the Congolese politicians in reaching the political settlement which they had achieved by the date of Independence was going to be taxed to the limit to find a way forward which would preserve a united Congo, and which would at the same time enable it to inspire sufficient confidence in the outside world that the Congo would be able to manage its affairs well enough for the world in general to be interested in helping it and investing in it. 'Belgium is bound to come badly out of all this,' I wrote the same day, 'although they will, in almost any conceivable circumstances, continue to have a major stake in the Congo. The government in Belgium and the Belgian people here seem to have lost their nerve. A panic chain-reaction has set in which can only be disastrous for Belgium and the Congo.'

Towards the end of July Lumumba set off for a two-and-a-half-week journey to North America, calling on the way at London and stopping briefly in two or three African countries—notably Ghana and Guinea. His departure and the virtual collapse of civil government, added to the reaction from the high level of excitement of the previous couple of weeks, produced a certain calm in Léopoldville. The fact that Lumumba could go away for so long at such a time was a measure of the incapacity of the man to face up to and try to cope with the situation in the Congo.

In this welcome period of peace and quiet it was possible for me (and other ambassadors similarly placed) to present my credentials to Kasavubu. I had become Ambassador instead of Consul-General when the Congo became independent. Normally, an ambassador is expected to remain more or less incognito until he has been received by the head of state: in the circumstances of July in Léopoldville, the Head of State had other more pressing affairs to attend to; and Congress of Vienna protocol was tacitly ignored by all concerned. However, the time had now come to put these things right; and, arrayed in my hot-weather uniform, complete with sword and helmet, I proceeded at a stately pace on 26 July to the residence of Kasavubu, which had been formerly the official residence of the Governor of Léopoldville province—the splendid house occupying a spectacular position overlooking the Congo river and the rapids below Léopoldville. It was as well that this appointment was not for an earlier date: our day had been made in early July when, with the wildest confusion around, a letter had arrived from a firm of Savile Row tailors informing me, 'We have been advised by the Foreign Office to supply you with only the Gold Russia, in order that you can add this to your existing Gorgets to make them to the Class required. The Russia is sewn on a ¼" from the edge of the Gorget. We enclose the Gold Russia herewith.' I was able, therefore, to be correctly dressed for the occasion.

It was a striking procession that we made with police outriders before and behind the open presidential car in which I rode; and two or three other cars as well. The populace, such as by then were again tentatively venturing out, clearly took fright as we approached. Cars and even a bus that came along swerved off the road on to the verge. Cyclists got off and pedestrians mostly were rooted to the spot. No one knew what such a manifestation of uniformed strength might portend: the bad days were too close at hand. Few, from lack of experience, could have guessed what in fact it was.

The only two Ambassadors who had already presented their credentials were the Belgian and the Ghanaian. It was not chance that this should have been so; in both cases this symbolized a false relationship which these two countries tried to establish with the Congo. Belgium, in negotiating a pre-Independence Treaty with the Congo (of which the legal validity was all along in doubt because it had never been ratified) had stipulated that the Belgian Ambassador to the Congo should always be *primus inter pares*. The Ghanaian, an unscrupulous and embittered racialist, whom Nkrumah presumably hoped could interpret his wishes in the Congo, had lost no time on arrival in going straight to Kasavubu and presenting him with his letter of appointment. This started him off on the wrong foot with the other Congolese whom he had ignored; and as he thereafter clung like a leech to Lumumba's side, it was not long before his uselessness became apparent and he was recalled—not before, however, he had been the instrument of passing on from Nkrumah to Lumumba some of the most perverse advice which could have been proffered. Some of the letters in which this advice was given were later published by the United Nations: their authenticity had been admitted at the time by the Ghana representative in Léopoldville. They provided obvious models for the letters printed in the Appendix.

By early August the pattern of events in those disastrous weeks of July became a little clearer. Two facts stood out: the trouble had been caused by the army and in no case were outrages committed by the civil population except when with rising unemployment they joined in the looting of abandoned Belgian houses, notably at Matadi and to a lesser extent in some other places. This was not an uprising of Africans against whites: it was by soldiers against their Belgian officers and in particular against the Flemish among them. At Thysville, for example, where the worst excesses were committed, the house of a European Salvation Army family was broken into by fifteen armed mutineers on the first night. They went all over the house, including the bathroom where the wife was in her bath. On being told, however, that the family were missionaries and were not Belgians, the soldiers quickly left. Secondly, fear on the part of the Belgians bred fear on the part of the mutinous Congolese Army, with the result that more and worse things happened than need have taken place if the Belgians had kept their heads.

The consequences of Belgian panic—'hysteria' as Hammarskjøld described it to me during his week's visit from the end of July—were aggravated by sudden ill-considered acts by the Belgian troops who had stayed behind in the Congo. These troops and their controlling authorities were naturally preoccupied with the danger to Belgian subjects; but, because of inadequate liaison, the Congolese were exceedingly jumpy at the slightest indication of movement by this relatively small number of Belgian troops, whose most valuable operation was the relief of the beleaguered group of Europeans in Luluabourg. That action was understandable; but the troops also made sudden descents on places where calm had been restored—sometimes days previously—shooting where they should have held their fire (e.g. at the port of Matadi), bombing from the air on wrong information, and so on. So deeply ingrained among the Congolese was fear of the power of Belgian soldiers that on one occasion in late July Lumumba broke up a Cabinet meeting at 11.30 p.m. and drove to the airport with several of his Ministers and a lorryload of troops because it had been rumoured that some Belgian soldiers had been seen there. After scouring the airport buildings, the only Belgian who could be found was the unfortunate chef of the restaurant, who was promptly arrested.

These weeks were indeed a calamitous revelation of Belgian morale and of their incapacity in both civil and military fields; and, as this had followed weeks and months of inept handling of political affairs, the relations between Belgium and the Congo touched bottom in that month of August. This development was marked by Lumumba's expulsion of the imposing Belgian Mission, ostensibly because of the use to which the remaining Belgian troops were being put at that time.

A further sharp and dangerous edge was given to the course of events in many centres by shortages which were discovered in the armouries of Force Publique depots when these were taken over by the new Congolese Army authorities. The hand-over was sometimes peacefully effected but sometimes followed unpleasant arrests and ill-treatment of Belgian officers. The missing arms were in some cases known, and in every case assumed, to have been handed out to the local Belgian civilians. This therefore led to frantic searches, by the mutinous Congolese Army troops, of houses, cars, and persons in order to recover arms. It was also widely known that Belgian civilians had kept themselves heavily armed ever since the January 1959 riots. Then again the whereabouts of all the weapons which were thus collected was not known; it was feared, however, that many had found their way into the hands of the African civil population. One thing, in fact, led to another, fanned by irresponsible propaganda over the radio, and produced the sorry debacle from which the world was having, painfully and expensively, to extract the Congo. All the time the wildest rumours mixed with the truth, which was itself impossible to establish at the time for lack of communications and lack of any civil authority. One often had to decide, like Poirot, from an armchair what the likely sequence and consequences of events had been or would be: after the first week of independence, no one knew for a time, from one day to the next, sometimes from one hour to the next, how things were going to develop.

By early August therefore the position was that a rapidly increasing U.N. military presence was showing itself all over the Congo except as yet in Katanga province. The first U.N. forces on the scene had been the Ghanaians, a small advance party being brought by Major-General Alexander, the Chief of Staff of the Ghana Army. Their presence in Léopoldville helped to contain the wilder manifestations of Congolese military indiscipline; but the atmosphere in the capital remained nervous for many weeks. U.N. troops did not have to shoot their way in anywhere, nor of course would they have been prepared to do so; on the contrary, they were practically everywhere welcomed. Almost with relief, the control of the armoury in Léopoldville was handed over to U.N. troops, and remained in their hands until Lumumba demanded its return to the Congolese Army. To the dismay of the U.N. military commanders, Bunche accepted this request and returned their store of arms to the Congolese troops. There were those, including Alexander and some of the U.N. civilian officials, who would have liked to see the U.N. disarm the Congolese Army altogether. This was an unrealistic approach to the problem. Perhaps it could have been done here and there, but it could not have been carried through everywhere; and the U.N. had neither the mandate to do this nor the competence to deal with the different kind of chaos that would have resulted. This was something which the Congolese and not the U.N. had to solve.

Stanleyville and some places in Orientale province proved exceptions to the general acceptance of the U.N. troops, when it looked as if the Ethiopian officer in command was not going to be strong enough to assert himself. But he succeeded, when many more Ethiopian troops had arrived, in establishing his authority and also setting up reasonably good working relations both with the civil authorities in the area, such as they were, and with the rump of the army. The U.N. troops were concerned with ensuring some sort of security in the main centres of population; and here and there, as in Orientale, they kept the main roads open for traffic. They were very limited, however, in what they could do when breaches of the peace occurred. The magistracy had disappeared. When a Ghanaian soldier caught a pickpocket red-handed in a Léopoldville street, the culprit could be taken as far as the police station, but the legal processes then ceased for lack of any means of prosecuting a case against him. Outside their strictly limited tasks, the U.N. troops were neither strong enough to interfere in Congolese affairs nor expected to do so. In Kasai province, sporadic fighting between the Lulua and the Baluba tribes again started with considerable loss of life and the atrocities which were by then common in the fighting between these two tribes. The U.N. troops, according to the report of their commander which General von Horn showed to me, had no intention of even trying to do anything about this; they regarded the quarrel, as indeed it was, as a matter for the Congolese authorities themselves.

While Lumumba was on his North American trip in August, Hammarskjøld passed through Léopoldville and was entertained to dinner by the Vice-Premier, Gizenga, at an open-air restaurant on one of the low hills outside Léopoldville. The U.N. had then been operating for a very few weeks in the Congo and already there had been some major clashes with Lumumba. There had indeed been real difficulties to resolve; and Ralph Bunche had at one time to face a threat from Lumumba, in one of his more irresponsible moments, to ask the U.N. to withdraw completely. But no one expected the virulent attack on the U.N. which was made by Vice-Premier Gizenga in his after-dinner speech, on the occasion of this large and formal dinner given in Hammarskjøld's honour. In well-chosen language and good French, he made a poisonous attack on both the U.N. and, by implication, on Hammarskjøld himself. While he spoke, copies of the speech were distributed to the guests by one of Lumumba's personal advisers, Mme Blouin, a half-French half-Guinean woman. Foreigners were embarrassed and Hammarskjøld was visibly upset. He made, however, a dignified and straightforward speech in reply; without attempting to argue about any of the particular points raised by Gizenga, he left the impression—as usual—of complete integrity of purpose, in startling contrast with the other's infirmity and dishonesty. This brief stop-over of Hammarskjøld's in Léopoldville was soon followed by the replacement of Bunche, whose health was not able to stand the increasing strain of the situation. His departure was a loss to the Congo and to the whole operation, and to the reputation of the United Nations in the Congo. This was so, even though it had become clear that he was not the person to be in control of the U.N.'s whole operation.

The problems of Katanga and the withdrawal of Belgian troops from the Congo were the two main questions, apart from matters of the U.N.'s own organization in the Congo, on which Hammarskjøld was engaged in negotiations with the Congolese government during his visits over the end of July and again for a few days from 11 August. The Congolese were insisting on the immediate withdrawal of all Belgian troops. Hammarskjøld said to me that these were the most difficult negotiations which he had ever conducted, 'and', he added, 'I have had many difficult negotiations'. He feared that unless Belgium unequivocally denounced Katanga separatism and co-operated with the U.N. by withdrawing its troops from Katanga as U.N. troops moved in, a very serious situation would arise both internally and internationally. Bunche had paid a brief visit to Katanga in early August but completely failed to get Tshombe's agreement to the stationing of U.N. troops there. A week later Hammarskjøld himself, his hand strengthened by the U.N. Resolution of 29 August again requesting the withdrawal of Belgian troops, went to Katanga. He persuaded Tshombe to allow a U.N. presence on condition that it did not interfere with Katangan internal affairs.

The end of July had passed without the serious labour troubles that were thought possible. As a precaution, a 6 p.m. curfew had been imposed in Léopoldville from 30 July; but there were no more signs of revolt by the civil population than there were during the mutiny in early July. The U.N. Food Relief Organization began distribution of food to the unemployed and to mothers with young children. Efforts were being concentrated on re-establishing the normal economic life of the country; and OTRACO, the state rail and river transport organization, was slowly reviving. Ships began to use Matadi port again, trains from Matadi to Léopoldville were functioning, and freight was again beginning to move up and down the river, although still only a small fraction of its previous volume. It would take several weeks either to entice back enough Belgians or to recruit sufficient other foreigners to enable OTRACO to approach the extent of its earlier business. And even that depended on a satisfactory settlement being reached with Katanga.

It is necessary from this point in time to distinguish between Belgian official policy towards the Congo before and immediately after Independence, and the attitudes of those many individual Belgians who were prepared to change their former ways and stay on or return to the Congo in a new relationship of friend and helper of the Congo. It took longer for the authorities, both governmental and business, back in Belgium, to make this change, and the process has not yet ceased; but the change began in the autumn of 1960 with the realization by Congolese leaders, even while Lumumba was still in power, that they needed Belgian help. The kind of love-hate relationship which most colonial connections seem to leave behind when the parting takes place was very much more acute, for a variety of reasons, in the case of Belgium/Congo than it normally has been between Great Britain and her ex-colonies. One of the shrewdest Belgians I ever met, the head of an important engineering group in the Congo, said to me some weeks before Independence that 'if, after a couple of years, they look on us as they do on you, just as another kind of foreigner, we shall have won out'. As the U.N. effort in the Congo grew, it became increasingly clear to the Congolese that the solution of their problems did not lie in that direction. The help of the Belgian government and many thousands of Belgian individuals was necessary: this was particularly so in the field of primary education where some knowledge of the many tribal languages—which the Belgians possessed—was as necessary as a knowledge of French itself. They were moreover used to living in remote areas.

During those early weeks of the U.N.'s involvement, a U.N. military presence began effectively to spread over the main inhabited centres of the Congo except in Katanga province; those weeks gave time also for the U.N. Headquarters to organize itself after the first chaotic fortnight when a wholly inadequate staff was attempting to plan its operations. These matters also occupied much of Hammarskjøld's time during his visit in August. I was told that he averaged one hour's sleep a night for his first five nights in Léopoldville.

By mid-August the security situation in the main towns was quiet on the surface; but there were great areas of the Congo where armed bands were free to roam as they liked. The U.N. forces were not intended or equipped or numerous enough to deal with local banditry; and the breakdown of communications was so widespread that there were no details available of conditions in many places and whole great areas. It was known, however, that the Lulua/Baluba hostilities in Kasai province continued unabated, with all the attendant misery and savagery which they had produced on earlier occasions. Among others who died in this way were several newly elected members of the Legislature and two Tunisian U.N. soldiers. Streams of Baluba refugees were trying to make their way to their tribal homelands in the southeast of the province, and the roads were strewn with abandoned—generally stolen—vehicles and corpses of humans and animals. Luluabourg, the capital, had about 150 Europeans remaining there instead of the usual four thousand; and many of the abandoned houses were being systematically broken into and pillaged. The railway station held insanitary numbers of refugees camping for days while they waited hopefully, but vainly, for trains to take them away. Even when trains did run they were stopped and sacked not many miles away. The economic life of the province was at a standstill and the new provincial government in effect gave up trying to govern. The Tunisian troops who had been posted there kept order of a sort in the town of Luluabourg and tried to arrange escorts for road convoys of refugees and a few trains. That was all they could attempt; and even the comparative security of the town was dependent on the continuance of a satisfactory liaison between the re-arming Congolese Army and the U.N. troops—a relationship which became daily more brittle. This picture repeated itself with local variations in the other provinces except Katanga, where the provincial government had fairly firm control over events.

So far as trade was concerned, the Congo slowly began to revive and river traffic resumed, although at a much slower pace, to some of the main centres such as the great Unilever plantations in the Kikwit area in Léopoldville province. Ordinary trade, however, outside the local radius was almost completely dead. No one knew how many of the goods depots throughout the country were still manned or even if they still existed, and traders were therefore reluctant to despatch goods from Léopoldville. Enormous debts were owing to head offices and firms in Léopoldville by their wholesale and retail agents throughout the Congo, many of whom (Belgians, Greeks, Portuguese, and Cypriots) had disappeared, while others could not be reached by ordinary postal services. Unilever, for example, in its various manifestations, had outstanding debts owed to it of well over £1 million sterling. Many smaller firms thus faced bankruptcy. These included even some quite large Belgian organizations whose head offices had never followed a policy of sending in money to the Congo to support their associate or subsidiary companies.

The administration of the Congo had been left suspended in the air with the departure of virtually all the senior officials in every department of government—at the centre, in the provinces, and in the districts. To give direction to a newly independent cabinet with ministers wholly inexperienced in this kind of life, with no tradition to draw upon to help them, no obvious bond to unite them, and no civil service machine behind them, was a daunting task. Although there were many capable Congolese, they were unable, because unprepared, to take over smoothly the running of a complicated machine. For example, only some 200 out of 600 doctors in the state medical services of the Congo remained in the country; and these were nearly all concentrated in the towns. Nearly all the nurses, however, who were mostly Roman Catholic nuns, remained, to their great honour, where they were. The first and major task of the World Health Organization (which was early on the scene) was to assist in the recruitment of medical teams and advise on the appointment of doctors who applied from all over the world to come to the Congo. It was also responsible for the placing of Red Cross medical teams from more than a dozen countries. None could be sent to remote areas where the insecurity was too great; but it began to look as if it would be possible to continue the work of the main hospitals in the towns without further dislocation. Soon health teams began spreading out and worked often in appallingly difficult circumstances and conditions. Public health matters were more difficult and things were obviously going to get steadily worse on this front. The problem of training Congolese doctors, the first of whom were only due to emerge from Lovanium University two years later, was almost

Paul Popper Ltd.

Paul Popper Ltd.

1. Joseph Kasavubu

2. Patrice Lumumba

3. Justin Bomboko (Foreign Minister), President Kasavubu, Clare
Timberlake (U.S. Ambassador), the author, and Lt.-Col. the Hon.
John Sinclair (British Military Attaché)

4. Russian propaganda portrayal of Lumumba

insuperable. There was a fairly numerous class of Congolese medical assistants who had done five years medical training (although of a kind which effectively prevented them from doing a further year or two and emerging as doctors); and they were capable of carrying out medical and surgical work not far short of what a qualified doctor could do. France gave valuable help in this important field of technical assistance and offered to take seventy-five of these men and arrange special three-year courses of instruction in five different French Universities. These courses were designed so that they could achieve full medical qualifications. The experiment went through successfully and I have no doubt produced a very valuable influx of qualified medical personnel. The W.H.O. set to work on a plan for a long-term association with the Congo which was to produce in the end 1,800 Congolese doctors. That the most successful part of the U.N.'s technical assistance was in the medical field was largely because of the personality of Doctor Bellerive who was appointed by the W.H.O. to take charge of its work in the Congo. This distinguished Haitian not only had already had a notable career in the W.H.O. but also had entirely the right attitude towards the Congolese. That is to say he came prepared to give of his best in order to help them, with no preconceived ideas as to his own, or his team's, superiority as educated outsiders over the local Congolese; and with the courage to take his own line in matters of official and personal relationships with the Congolese authorities. One of his first acts was to remove his own office outside the U.N.'s Headquarters, which rapidly became a symbol of the uneasy relationship between the U.N. and the Congolese.

Similar serious problems faced the Ministry of Education. About one thousand Belgian school-teachers had left the Congo and there were no Congolese able to take their places. The new Minister of Education set about trying to negotiate with the teachers in Belgium the conditions under which some of them at any rate would be prepared to return. The lack of trained teachers had the additional effect that it prevented many Belgian families from returning, who might otherwise have thought of coming back, because their children could not be educated. A UNESCO team therefore tried to do for education what the W.H.O. were striving for in the medical field, but did not achieve the same success. A much-publicized offer by UNESCO in the summer of 1960 to find 1,600 teachers to replace Belgians proved to be a failure. The figure fell rapidly and steadily to a few hundred, but even to fill that number of vacancies it was very difficult for UNESCO to recruit qualified teachers who were prepared to go where Belgian teachers had been content to live and work; and it was not satisfactory to recruit teachers on a short-term contract, as this meant that very soon most of them began looking to the day when they could leave the Congo. Nor, although no doubt this was specified in the recruitment arrangements, did all the teachers speak comprehensible French, which was the only common language of the Congo. One particular group of ten, including a Spaniard and some Chinese graduates of the Sorbonne, was sent to Luluabourg. The next day, the Spaniard had to be evacuated in a hurry because, having drunk too much the night before and danced a mock bull-fight in the street, he was thought to be a Belgian paratrooper in disguise; and after two days teaching by the Chinese, the students went diffidently to the U.N. representative and asked whether they could not be supplied with someone who would teach them in French. So the Chinese had to be returned. In fact, many Belgian teachers did come back in the autumn, and over the succeeding months many more returned.

In the general administrative services in the provinces the official Belgian estimate at this time was that some twenty per cent of the Belgian civil servants had remained, although how many of these intended to continue was not known. Thus it was quite clear that there would be a serious deterioration in the standards of administration owing to the lack of qualified Congolese replacements for all those who had left and the virtual impossibility of replacing a significant proportion of them by nationals of other countries. An important example of the difficulties facing the Congo in those early weeks and months was the slowing-up of the transport system. OTRACO had employed until 30 June some 1,200 Belgians. Forty remained behind in July; and a new Board and Director-General, wholly Congolese, were appointed. The new head of the organization had not only worked in it for twenty-eight years as a clerk but was a thoroughly competent and independent-minded person. He decided that the Congolese could not run this great enterprise—particularly on the engineering, maintenance, and accounts sides—without the help of a considerable number of the former Belgian employees. He told me that he wanted to engage about 250 of them— he did not need the rest; it was known that OTRACO had been over-manned by Belgians in the past. He knew the individuals whom he wanted, essential qualifications being not only their technical and administrative competence but their ability to work with Congolese. To help in his recruitment campaign he engaged a retired Belgian

Director-General of OTRACO in Brussels to interview candidates for him in Belgium. He failed to get any support at all from the U.N. for this programme; the U.N. Headquarters in Léopoldville were resolutely against the return to the Congo of any Belgian in any position of authority: a Belgian to the U.N. chiefs indeed was like a communist to Joseph McCarthy. When the new head of OTRACO came up against this hurdle, he decided to go ahead against the opposition of the U.N. in the Congo, and proceeded to do so. He scouted the U.N.'s idea of bringing in for him numbers of experts from various countries, and by the time we left, a year later, he had recruited 175 of the Belgians whom he wanted.

The supreme example of the need for reorganization and training was in the Army, now without a defined task, without effective discipline, and without experienced officers. Only the Commander-in-Chief, Lundula, his Chief of Staff, Mobutu, and the Commandant of Léopoldville garrison had been confirmed in their appointments; all other officer nominations throughout the country were provisional. Moreover, the confusion in the Army was made even greater by the expulsion from Katanga of the thousands of soldiers stationed there who belonged by origin to other provinces. This break-up of the Congolese Army's former carefully devised racial-mixing system was the result of Tshombe's wish to ensure that he kept only Katangan soldiers in Katanga. He felt that he would be more certain of the support of the Army if its members had no roots or affiliations elsewhere. The obvious need, therefore, was to select and train as rapidly as possible a new officer corps. Mobutu set about this at once and arranged, with Lumumba's approval and as an addition to other training schemes, to send a batch of cadets to the United Kingdom for a crash programme of training—he had declined Nkrumah's invitation to send 100 young men to Ghana for training. At the very last minute, news of this British training assistance reached Hammarskjöld in New York. He appealed to Macmillan (then Prime Minister and visiting New York) to cancel the arrangements, and for a variety of reasons Macmillan acceded to his request. At 5 o'clock one morning, therefore, as the group of young Congolese soldiers was literally on the tarmac about to enter their transport plane to go to Britain, we had to inform them that the whole thing was off and that they must return to barracks. The U.N., under pressure from Egypt, similarly blocked a request from the Congolese Army for training facilities in Israel. Mobutu then arranged for much larger numbers to be trained in Belgium; again the U.N.

objected. But in this case both Mobutu and the Belgian government were prepared to ignore these objections, and hundreds were sent— sometimes with the knowledge (although not the agreement) of the U.N., and sometimes without. From the Congolese point of view this was obvious sense. A proposal for a mixed-manned training establishment for officers, run by the U.N. in the Congo, never got off the ground. Mobutu knew what he wanted and he went ahead to get it by sending his young cadets to Belgium. Several hundred left in 1960 and 1961, some for a full and rigorous three-year course. One difficulty which soon became apparent with these new young officers was how they were to fit in, on their return, with the much older senior officers who had newly been promoted from the ranks. This problem had not been resolved by the time I left; but it looked then as if the only practical solution would be to form completely new units in which all the young officers would serve, with, in the early years, very carefully selected senior officers who had reached their positions without any officer training.

In all those and other fields, it was only the Belgians who were able and willing to attempt the long haul which was required to help the Congo on to its independent feet. And provided the Belgians who returned to the Congo in any official capacity were those whom the Congolese liked and accepted, there should have been nothing but help for this from the U.N. Such, however, was not the case. On his return from a visit to New York in the late summer of 1960, I called on Rajeshwar Dayal, who had replaced Bunche as head of the United Nations Organization in the Congo (UNOC), and this matter came up. He told me of the obstructiveness which his office had experienced from some individual Belgians in different Congolese Ministries and spoke bitterly about Belgium. He would not accept my view that the Belgians were the best placed to bring to the Congo the kind of assistance which was so desperately needed, and that, instead of forbidding it, the U.N. should encourage it, subject to necessary safeguards. I suggested that he ask for a senior Belgian official, perhaps from the Ministry of Justice, to be seconded from Brussels to his staff and given the sole task of investigating complaints by UNOC against Belgian officials in the Congo. If such a person were given, I said, the power to repatriate at once any Belgian who to his satisfaction had been abusing his position in this way, I thought that it would only be necessary for two or three to be expelled for the rest to toe the line. Dayal, however, refused to contemplate this kind of solution and remained rabidly anti-Belgian.

All this time a multitude of problems had pressed upon Lumumba and his government. These varied from Tshombe's declared secessionist intentions to the arrival of representatives and observers from nearly all the countries of the world on the Congo's doorstep. Lumumba completely lacked the sort of statesmanship which would have been able to work out a suitable solution with Tshombe. It had to be all or nothing, at once. This was unfortunate; there was nothing sacrosanct in the constitution of the Congo which the Belgians had bequeathed to the new state. It could have been and has since been several times altered. Personal jealousies and ambitions, however, drove Lumumba to try and assert his will against Tshombe, and the use of force to do so was all that he could think of. The Congolese troops whom Lumumba ordered to advance against Katanga, which could only be reached through Kasai province, at a time when a very uneasy truce existed between the two Kasai tribes, were opposed—because they came with Julua support—by the Baluba tribesmen. These had been withdrawing into South Kasai and grouping under Kalonji, with their backs to Katanga. Additional butchery was thus superimposed on the savage fighting which had already taken place in that region; and chaos spread with the execution of hundreds of tribal chiefs and other opponents of Lumumba's political ambitions. Lumumba's brother, a trained communist and now a political leader in this area, assisted the process. The Congolese Army failed to break through to Katanga, but not before many thousands of casualties had been caused in bitter and brutal fighting. A Red Cross doctor stated in late August that he had himself counted 1,400 bodies, mainly Baluba. Other more immediately pressing problems claimed Lumumba's attention at this time and the Congolese Army was soon recalled from its abortive attempt to conquer Katanga. The Balubas, however, were later to get their revenge.

It was for the new independent Congo to make its own decision about how it should be represented in foreign countries, and many people, particularly Belgians, hoped that Lumumba would invite Belgium to act for the Congo until his country could organize its own diplomatic and consular service. But Lumumba went his own way and chose otherwise. He invited Nkrumah, for example, to allow the Ghana Embassy in Moscow to act for the Congo in Russia; and by the end of August, 784 visas had been issued in Moscow for the Congo. This was only one, though perhaps the most striking, of the results of independence in the international field. Foreign embassies and consulates dealt mainly with the Congolese Foreign Minister, Bomboko, who was both able and friendly, and with whom it was a pleasure to do business. But, on occasion, the Ambassadors needed also to meet Lumumba, and this introduced a new dimension to his life.

On his return from the North American trip he had been confronted with increasing political confusion superimposed on general administrative disintegration. While he had been away, opposition and regrouping of Congolese political leaders, together with frustrating delays and ineffectiveness in many directions, led to increasing opposition to his own position. Not only had the Katanga situation hardened against him but his centralizing ambitions had stimulated again the desire of the ABAKO party for its own province in the Lower Congo— a demand which had only with great difficulty been overcome a few weeks earlier by the formation of a coalition government for the whole of the province. And it was not only in Kasai that a separate state was being proclaimed (by Kalonji), but in the Équateur province the activities of Bolikango and others (including, unfortunately, the acting Belgian Consul-General, who was rash enough to put on paper a scheme of separatism for the provincial government) all reflected ideas of federalism which were totally opposed to Lumumba's conception of a strong unitary state. At Lumumba's first meeting with Parliament after his return, he faced a hostile audience; but in a speech of about one and a half hours he completely converted them to the point where they gave him practically unanimous support. This enabled him to reverse a typically irresponsible decision which he had made: just before leaving on his travels he had signed away the entire mineral rights of the Congo for a sum, which was said to have been £750 million, to a well-known international financier. This was now repudiated on his return, and the first of the endlessly complicated negotiations with powerful Belgian interests was started.

Although Lumumba apparently regained much of his authority with his colleagues, he did not fully do so, and showed himself nervous and jumpy in the process. He suppressed criticism by the method of arresting journalists, closing down the Belga and Agence France-Presse news agencies, establishing a censorship of incoming newspapers, and so on. At the same time, he was trying to re-equip the army from armouries guarded by U.N. troops and persuaded Bunche to authorize the return of their arms to the Congolese forces. He also wished to take back control of Léopoldville airport from the United Nations. He was angry and frustrated because Hammarskjøld would not agree to facilitate his entry into Katanga by giving him United Nations troops for this purpose. It looked indeed for a time as if he would accept the offer of troops from member countries of the United Nations who were willing to help him personally to establish his position. A Russian contribution, for example, of 80 lorries and 14 aircraft was at his personal disposition, instead of being under the United Nations Force Commander as the United Nations Resolutions required. The lorries kept us awake one night on their arrival to line up next door for Lumumba's inspection. That was from 1 to 3 a.m. Lumumba saw them at dawn and they left at once to help his troops in Kasai. The intemperate letters which he wrote to Hammarskjøld at this period showed that he felt time to be not on his side, and proved his incapacity to face up to the real problems and difficulties of finding a satisfactory constitutional framework for the Congo. This needed different qualities from those of the skilful political manipulator which was all that he had hitherto shown himself to be. He was driven also to make the most of the threat caused by Belgian troops being in the country and tried desperately to strengthen his position by flogging that dead horse: full agreement had been reached by this time on the withdrawal of the Belgian troops.

It was not easy to see how this situation could be resolved. I put forward a suggestion to London that the U.N. might consider taking a political initiative to help in resolving the crisis, just as it had taken a military initiative in the previous month. I strongly believed that the finding of a political compromise between the centralists and the federalists was essentially a Congolese problem. I equally felt that at that time a lasting solution could be more easily reached if some skilled assistance was offered from outside. In the last week of August, a conference of African states took place in Léopoldville, in a desperate effort by them to bring some such help and counsel to Lumumba. Congo developments were bringing all the African states into disrepute, sometimes even ridicule. Something had to be done by his fellow Africans, and this conference was therefore arranged. Lumumba, conscious that he was not cutting the figure that he would wish to, absented himself from Léopoldville for three days, when he visited Stanleyville in the middle of the conference. This was to avoid the chorus of criticism which most of these African leaders were prepared to make. When the conference broke up on 31 August it had achieved, in effect, nothing. The Sudanese delegate told me that he had proposed that a conference committee go to Katanga to discover from Tshombe what his real intentions were, and to try to reach a solution. This proposal had got so

far as to be agreed by all members of the conference except the Congolese representatives themselves. This was not Lumumba's formula.

After his return Lumumba plunged at once into ever more and more
business. The last time I saw him, late in August, he had two other
visitors sitting in his office, his secretary standing beside him trying to
get an urgent signature, two telephones on his desk which rang about
a dozen times in the ten minutes that I was with him, and in front of
him a huge pile of files which he was trying to work through. He
looked as if he had not slept the night before; and indeed it was by then
widely known that he could only carry on by taking drugs. There was
a kind of glaze in his eyes, together with an inability to concentrate,
certainly on the particular matter which I was trying to discuss with
him. Part of the trouble was that he was wholly unable to delegate
authority; and indeed perhaps had no one whom he felt he could fully
trust. He had surrounded himself with a small selection of intimate
advisers which included a Belgian lawyer, Mme Blouin (the Guinea
lady), and one or two others who had suddenly appeared on the scene.
Some of these had communist affiliations. He was all the time receiving
from Nkrumah a stream of advice—so voluminous that I doubt whether
he had time to read it all, and so bad that it could only encourage him
in foolish courses (some of these harmful letters were subsequently
published in a U.N. document). It was not to be wondered at, therefore, that he soon found himself in a situation which he could not
master.

7

The full support given to Hammarskjøld by the Security Council meeting of 21 August had strengthened the hands of the U.N. authorities and forced Lumumba to discard all idea of an appeal for military help outside the context of the U.N. The withdrawal of the Belgian troops began also to take the edge from an apparently endless succession of incidents, involving mainly Belgians, which had made life for the rest of us only less uncomfortable in August than it had been in July. In the course of the month many Belgians paid for the continued presence in the Congo of their compatriots in the army by being arrested or expelled, and Congolese/Belgian relations sank to their lowest level. After relations had been broken off, only two junior clerks remained out of all the staffs of the Belgian Embassy and Consulates-General throughout the country. The slow-motion political crisis continued up to 5 September.

That evening Kasavubu went to the radio station and announced in a brief broadcast that he had dismissed Lumumba, as he was entitled under the law to do, and had appointed Ileo to succeed him. This followed fairly strong private criticism of Lumumba's conduct of affairs which he had made in the previous few days. By ordinary standards it was an incredibly incompetent coup d'état; but Kasavubu was like this. At one time he had sent for the acting head of UNOC to ask him how a coup d'état should be organized. Having made the announcement that Ileo was in future to be regarded as the Prime Minister, Kasavubu returned home and went to bed, having taken no precautions whatever to see the thing through. He had even left behind on the table in the radio station the text of his short announcement. Lumumba found it there an hour later and was able to announce that it had not been countersigned by any responsible Minister. Three broadcasts during the night by Lumumba induced Kasavubu the next day to order his arrest; but again he did nothing to see that this was carried out, and it was a full week before Lumumba was taken away to the military camp in Léopoldville and confronted by the Public Prosecutor. It did not take him long to talk himself out of that situation, nor to order the arrest of the Public Prosecutor for his impudence. Meanwhile, U.N.

forces had taken control of Léopoldville airport and had temporarily put the radio station off the air—both actions designed to limit the possible ill effects of the new constitutional developments. Kasavubu had a naive belief that because he felt that he was in the right in this constitutional struggle, he was bound to win. The curious thing is, of course, that he did; and that from 5 September Lumumba's power began to wane. As the days went by there was a steady swing in the Congolese Army in favour of Kasavubu; but there were no signs of the ability of Ileo's government to act with the determination which would secure the support of the people who had been disillusioned by Lumumba and were waiting to be rallied behind his successor. Who was, during those days, the legal Prime Minister of the Congo was hardly relevant; the constitutional law had been provisional and unadopted. It was followed by Lumumba when it suited him as a matter of practice, and was the subject of great legal argument. This unsatisfactory confusion continued until 14 September, with a prolonged battle going on throughout with communiqués, press conferences, and legalistic, journalistic, and parliamentary argument. No blood was shed except in the concluding phases of the military action ordered by Lumumba against the Baluba tribe and Katanga. None of the people who were arrested on one charge or another stayed in prison for longer than a day or two, nor were they brought to trial. Lumumba, claiming still to be Prime Minister, used his active information apparatus to the full while Kasavubu remained silent and inactive.

In this unusual stalemate between a perpetually moving force and a motionless object, Mobutu, then Army Chief of Staff, intervened. With a small bodyguard of military police he appeared, unannounced, on the evening of 14 September in a popular bar, and stated that the Army had taken over power and suspended all politicians and political activity until the end of the year. He had broadcast, immediately before, an announcement to the same effect. The machinery of government, he added, was to be conducted by eleven Commissioners-General, who would be from the intellectual élite of the Congo who had mostly studied abroad. Kasavubu, Lumumba, Ileo and the other politicians had been 'neutralized', and the sitting of the Assembly suspended. Russian and Czech technicians and diplomats would be ordered out of the Congo and help would be accepted only through the United Nations. Action to implement these policies was taken with surprising speed and efficiency. The Palais de la Nation was sealed off by well-turned-out and polite military police (in contrast with the often slovenly and offensive sentinels who had hitherto been on guard there); and a few half-hearted attempts by resentful parliamentarians to assemble were easily thwarted. The Commissioners-General were duly nominated and on 20 September took over their allotted offices without incident. The residences of Kasavubu and Lumumba were both put under a heavy guard of U.N. and Congolese Army troops.

Lumumba was confined to comparative inactivity and rumours of his arrest and threats to his life by some enraged Baluba soldiers proved unfounded; he was saved by U.N. troops from the possibility of this when he went to see Mobutu immediately after the announcement on 14 September—but he was reported to have lost on that occasion some very damning documents which he was carrying. The leading newspaper in Léopoldville, the *Courrier d'Afrique*, published letters alleged to have been obtained in this way. Two are printed in translation in the Appendix (see also Plate 5). I was not convinced at the time of their genuineness; nor have I been since. But whether or not they were forgeries, the point is that they were published in the press and were widely believed to be actual letters from Lumumba; they do reflect— and this is my reason for reproducing them—policies and, in some cases, practices for which Lumumba and, later in Stanleyville his lieutenant Gizenga must be held responsible.

The army under Mobutu had the situation in Léopoldville under control, at least in respect of law and order and the neutralization of the politicians. Mobutu also seemed to be getting his authority accepted by army units elsewhere in the Congo. The Soviet bloc representatives were given sufficient time only to enable their departure to be seemly if rapid. They accepted the decision and made immediate preparations, spending the whole of one night burning large quantities of paper. They feared indeed that their previous activities under Lumumba's régime would lead to physical attack on their Embassy in the different circumstances prevailing when General Mobutu had taken over power. The Russian Ambassador appeared in the U.N. Headquarters in the middle of the night to ask for additional U.N. military protection against the guard which had been put on the Embassy by the Congolese Army, even though the soldiers had shown not the slightest sign of doing anything except prevent further contact with the Embassy. In making this panic appeal at 2 a.m. the Russian Ambassador let out also that he thought he might well be sent to Siberia on his return to Russia, because he had failed in his mission. The Russians left the following day; and not only from Léopoldville. Wherever they were, they scrammed and fled (for example from Stanleyville) over any border which they could reach. They took away the aircraft which they had just presented to the Congo, with the paint still wet where they obliterated the new Congolese designation of the planes. Many of the departing Russians went to Ghana, although I never knew what ultimately happened to the Ambassador himself. But the departure of all those Russians took place without, so far as I am aware, the slightest personal inconvenience or molestation—granted of course that it is unpleasant to have to pack up and leave in a day or two. The contrast with the departure shortly afterwards of Nkrumah's representative was marked.

Mobutu, with Kasavubu's full backing, went on with a careful process of snipping off the tentacles through which Lumumba had been able to control and direct the power inherited with his office. Twenty members of Lumumba's entourage were arrested; and it had become known that warrants were out for the arrest of Gizenga (the Vice-Prime Minister), two other Ministers, and a number of other individuals, as well as for Lumumba's own arrest. The French press secretary to Lumumba left the country, together with Mme Blouin, then holding the designation of Chief of Protocol in the Prime Minister's Office; they left hurriedly for Ghana at the same time as the Russians. This slow process of attrition went on satisfactorily and the daily question was whether Lumumba himself would be arrested. He was still under U.N. and Congolese guard in his own house—the latter in an outer ring to try and ensure that Lumumba did not escape with U.N. connivance. There were reports of reconciliation between him and Kasavubu, presumably on the ground that Kasavubu had also been immobilized; and the representatives of some African states, as well as the U.N. Headquarters itself, all tried their hand at effecting this. But Kasavubu made it consistently clear that he would not accept Lumumba as Prime Minister; and although he did not leave his own residence, he received a considerable stream of visitors and held a succession of meetings in it. In particular, he was in continuous close consultation with Mobutu and with Bomboko—the latter had at one point been dismissed by Lumumba, reappointed by Ileo, and had then been nominated as chairman of his Commissioners by Mobutu.

At the beginning, Mobutu's military coup d'état seemed no more likely to produce an effective government than Kasavubu's nomination of Ileo after the dismissal of Lumumba. But within a week Mobutu had secured effective control in the capital and, despite his declaration that his only political action would be to 'neutralize' the politicians, he won over, or drove into the background, many of Lumumba's supporters and more than once was on the point of taking the decisive step of seizing their leader. A number of factors combined to deter him. His own character was not cast in the dictator's mould and he seemed at that time to have no real liking for his military role. He shared the general Congolese aversion to taking the final irrevocable step while the slightest chance of compromise or further discussion remained. He was of a stable character, intelligent, and, as I found in all my many dealings with him, friendly and honourable.

The Ghana representative took the lead in open support of Lumumba. Djin, the first Ghana Ambassador, had frequently attended meetings of Lumumba's Cabinet. He was succeeded by Nathaniel Welbeck, another extremist Ghanaian, who was prepared to follow Nkrumah in straining the purpose of the U.N. in the Congo to suit his leader's personal ambitions. The Ghana brigade commander with the U.N. forces indeed said that he had received orders from Nkrumah not only to protect Lumumba's person from harm but to prevent his arrest, even if by so doing Ghana troops had to act in contradiction to their orders from the U.N. Headquarters. The brigade commander added, however, that he would follow U.N. instructions and not any political directive from Accra. So obstructive were the activities of Nkrumah's agents that Mobutu demanded the removal of the Ghana and Guinea troops.

It was especially unfortunate that resentment against the Ghanaian forces should have been created, because their military conduct had been exemplary in conditions that had often been difficult, and the behaviour and bearing of all ranks had been most praiseworthy. Brigadier Michel, who died not long afterwards in an air accident outside Accra airport, was a fine officer whom we had come to know well, and his death was a loss not only to Ghana but to all Africa. My wife has a letter from him thanking her for organizing and operating a mobile canteen for the Ghana troops. She did this from early August when the troops had no access to shops or the kind of personal supplies such as sweets, stationery, and so on, to which they were accustomed; and they had no common language with the Congolese. Her mobile store, in a huge truck lent by Unilever, and with a Congolese and Ghanaian soldier sitting beside the driver, went round the various camps of the Ghana forces in Léopoldville and seemed to meet a much-felt need. It ended in late September when the Ghanaian troops were about to move away from Léopoldville. Months later my wife got a charming letter from a Ghanaian sergeant telling her how much the mobile canteen had meant to the soldiers and ending, 'Let me assure you that the phrase "out of sight, out of mind" can have no meaning with us for wherever any conversation on Léopoldville is held, you will be remembered.' A popular British newspaper captioned a photograph of this canteen in action with the phrase 'Envoy's wife delivers the goods.'

Moroccan influence had a certain effect on the conduct of the U.N. operations, and Major General Kettani, who was the U.N.'s deputy supreme commander, was charged also with the special task of planning the reorganization of the Congolese Army and for a brief time was the military adviser to Lumumba. In those weeks one of Morocco's chief interests was to influence the development of Mauritanian independence; and by supporting Ghana-Guinea policy in the Congo, it looked as if Morocco was hoping to get the support of those states in quite another field. At all events, the Moroccan influence was cast on the side of supporting Lumumba's claim to be the legitimate Prime Minister, even after Kasavubu had dismissed him and, later, General Mobutu had appointed his Commissioners.

The rest of the Congo was not seriously affected by the political manoeuvrings in the capital. They had plenty of their own incidents: for example, when the troops received their pay in Stanleyville in September, they promptly arrested their officers because they considered that the officers had received an undue proportion of the money which had arrived—an additional complication was that 1¼ million francs of it had been stolen on the way by air from Léopoldville. Fighting had stopped in Kasai province and all was peaceful in Katanga, where Tshombe was in full control of the south-east part of the province which contained the principal mineral reserves. From this position of comparative strength, he made it clear that he would not have dealings with any Congolese government which included Lumumba. In many places, of course, the provincial administrative machinery had collapsed and there were huge areas where security and public order were non-existent; some of the W.H.O. medical teams ran into trouble on this account when they reached the remoter areas. The general picture was one of muddle and confusion, waiting for some sort of strong government at the centre to take up the reins and to find an acceptable basis for relations between the centre and the provinces. 'It was not just a problem to be solved by the re-establishment of personal relations between two or three people,' wrote the *Courrier d'Afrique*, the only daily paper appearing regularly in Léopoldville. 'It is a much deeper problem of concern to six provinces and 14 million people. Those who limit themselves to a simple reconciliation have completely failed to understand the Congo crisis.'

By 1 October a total of twenty-eight Commissioners had been appointed under their chairman, Bomboko, who was also Commissioner-General for Foreign Affairs and in that capacity paid a brief visit to New York. These Commissioners continued to receive the support of Kasavubu and were reluctantly accepted by the U.N. Headquarters as the authority with which it could do day-to-day business, although not as the legal government of the country.

Undeterred by physical assaults on two of their members by some of Lumumba's Youth Movement on 26 September, the College of Commissioners, as they were collectively styled, issued a statement on 3 October defining their powers and formally accepting the responsibility entrusted to them by Mobutu. This was stated to be entirely technical and provisional because they had no mandate from the people and had not been elected. They disclaimed any desire to take political power, their objective being to keep the administrative machine running so that whatever government emerged from a round table conference, which they were charged with arranging, would find a working administration. They declared that the economic crisis was one of their most urgent concerns, followed closely in importance by the need to reopen schools and the courts of justice. In matters of foreign policy, they proclaimed solidarity with all African nations who were against Western or Russian colonialism or neo-colonialism. They expressed gratitude to the African countries which had helped the Congo but 'would never accept that certain of these countries, few in number, should profit from circumstances to meddle in our internal affairs and impose policies which are not those of the Congolese people. The Ghanaians and Guineans have been and remain our brothers but our relations must be established on a basis of mutual respect for our national sovereignty.' To the U.N. Organization they expressed thanks for help and acknowledged that one of the difficulties for the U.N. mission was the problem they themselves were finding in organizing authority. They therefore offered the U.N. a formula for collaboration which would prevent the paralysis of government but would also ensure that Congolese authority would not be subservient to the U.N. The declaration of the Commissioners ended by stating that the U.N. should deal with them on matters of finance and economics, supply, education, communications, and transport; and that their mandate was strictly limited to these fields and to the duration of the political crisis.

The main line of approach by the Commissioners to the political crisis was their plan, supported both by Kasavubu and Ileo, for a roundtable meeting of all the country's political leaders. They suggested that perhaps ten from each province should attend. Arrangements were put in the hands of a committee of five of the Commissioners. Reactions from the most prominent of the politicians varied: Lumumba denounced the whole affair and said that he would boycott it; Kalonji, who was busy getting himself crowned as King of the Balubas in their part of Kasai, accepted the idea but stated that he would not sit at the same table as Lumumba; and Tshombe accepted it with the qualification that the meeting should be held on neutral ground and that Lumumba should hold no position of authority. Bolikango, who had been Minister of Information in Ileo's brief government and had been doing most of the public propaganda against Lumumba, suggested that the meeting should be held in another African country. A group of twenty-six young army representatives was sent by Mobutu to canvass the round table conference idea in the provinces, but general opinion was sceptical of the chances that it would ever take place. If it did, it was felt, it could produce nothing more constructive than one more government to add to those already claiming existence.

On 2 October a significant event marked the further erosion of Lumumba's position. At a meeting of citizens of Orientale province (Lumumba's own base) which was held in Léopoldville, six Deputies of Lumumba's provincial party denounced him for his dealings with communism and for his responsibility for the country's economic and political chaos. These dissidents included Songolo, who had been Minister of Communications in Lumumba's Cabinet, and others who had not before openly criticized their leader. The following day a lengthy and violent condemnation of Lumumba was issued by the same group. It demanded as an indispensable condition that Lumumba be removed from power and added that the signatories of that declaration intended to tour Orientale province in order to 'unmask the communist traitor'. A more personal blow came when both Lumumba's younger brother and the Governor of Orientale province, a supporter of Lumumba, were placed under house arrest by the Congolese Army in Stanleyville.

While the attrition of Lumumba's position continued slowly, Mobutu directed his attention to the armed forces. He was deeply disappointed

RÉPUBLIQUE DU CONGO

Léopoldville, le 15 septembre 1960.

N° STRICTEMENT CONFIDENTIEL.

CABINET
DU PREMIER MINISTRE

OBJET:
Mesures d'application de la
première phase de la dicta-
ture.

1 annexe.

A Monsieur F I N A N T
Président Provincial du Gouvernement
à STANLEYVILLE. -

Cher Monsieur,

Je vous fais tenir en annexe, l'exemplaire
vous destiné de ma lettre circulaire de ce jour, relative à l'objet
repris en marge.

Pour cause de confiance, je retarde l'expé-
dition des exemplaires destinés à vos Collègues. Je le ferai dès que
possible.

Comme toute la Province Orientale est entre
NOS MAINS, vous pourriez déjà vous mettre au travail en exécutant
soigneusement les ordres donnés.

Je vous promets tout mon appui au cas où cer-
taines personnes voudraient intervenir pour vous faire des critiques
de quelque nature que ce soit.

N'oubliez pas d'encourager continuellement nos
camarades éparpillés dans la Province, en leur affirmant que con-
formément à la convention, le CONGO deviendra ce qu'ils nous ont
demandé.

Enfin, dans votre programme d'arrestation des
membres de l'opposition et autres, il convient de commencer par les
plus effluents; comme par exemple, KUPA François, LOPES Antoine,
EDINDALI André, TABALO.J.,MOTTA..., tous les grands chefs et
même certains de vos collaborateurs (membres du Gouvernement provincial) qui essayeront de vous critiquer.

En procédant de la sorte, tout le monde à Stanleyville aura peur de Votre Autorité comme on en a de la mienne ici
à Léopoldville. Ainsi, nous finirons par conduire tous les habitants
de la République par le bout du nez comme les brebis, en commen-
çant bien entendu par la Province Orientale qui est déjà chose acquise
à nos camarades de l'Orient qui, sous l'étiquette "techniciens" ont
commencé à jeter malignement et d'une manière sûre, les premiers
appâts de notre doctrine.

La présente confirme mes
ordres verbaux antérieurs.
N.B. -N'oubliez pas que c'est
grâce aux menaces graves
que je lance à tout moment
que la balance politique s'in-
cline favorablement de notre côté.

Mettez-vous immédiatement au travail et courage.
VIVE L'UNION SOVIETIQUE. VIVE KROUTCHEV

Le Premier Ministre

P. LUMUMBA. -

5. Letter from Lumumba as reproduced in the *Courrier d'Afrique*,
Léopoldville. (See p. 81 and Appendix (1) for translation).

86]

6. At the Nigerian Independence Day party in the garden of the British Ambassador's residence, Léopoldville, 1 October 1960

7. General Mobutu and the author

and bitterly critical of the U.N. for their suspicion at the last minute of his plan to send Congolese Army cadets for training in the U.K. His views on U.N. interference were not improved by the announcement of a U.N. spokesman, without any prior consultation with him, that a U.N. military training school would be set up in Luluabourg. This produced an explosive reaction in the form of a statement to the press, and an equally firm statement on the same lines from the Commissioner-General for Defence. Both stated that the U.N. had no right arbitrarily to determine how or where army training should be conducted, and emphasized the Congolese desire and intention that training should be done abroad in countries selected by Congolese authorities and that a military academy would be set up in due course by themselves. A head-on collision between the Congolese and the U.N. Mission was therefore approaching. This was to some extent induced by the return of Bomboko, who had been frustrated in New York in his desire to be seated in the U.N. as the legal representative of the Congo. The stiffening of the Congolese attitude to U.N. interference in Congolese internal affairs coincided with the steadily increasing authority of Mobutu over the whole Congolese Army. At an outspoken press conference on 11 October Bomboko said that the Congolese had no intention of getting rid of Belgian imperialism and then of falling under the rule of another brand of (black) imperialism. The pressure of Ghana, Guinea, the United Arab Republic, and other such states on the U.N. policy followed in the Congo (in particular urging U.N. support of Lumumba) was creating a dangerous situation. There was no doubt that the U.N. policy of favouring Lumumba for wider reasons of world politics was making steadily more difficult the solution of the Congo's internal constitutional and political crisis.

When the Commissioners had been at work for a few weeks, Kasavubu went to New York (accompanied by Bomboko) to assert his position as Head of State with the U.N. Assembly and to secure the seating of *his* delegation as the Congo's representatives, rather than Lumumba's nominees. Great objection was taken by a number of Afro-Asian representatives and procedural obstruction was employed to the full. But Kasavubu in the end secured recognition and had a triumphal return to Léopoldville. He emerged from the aircraft, after some delay, in a brand new general's uniform; and a military parade on 17 November was, in its way, a further assertion of the Congo's independence. The U.N. authorities had orders to prevent this parade from taking place, but of course were not able to do so. On 27 November Kasavubu gave

T.H.—7

a large and formal dinner party, when I was seated between Kasavubu and his wife, and my wife between Kasavubu and Mobutu. A good speech was made by the Commissioner of Finance, an able and lucid young man. Kasavubu spoke simply and quietly in his reply, in which he said, 'We need help and technicians, but they are to help us. The Congo will choose its technicians where it likes. The U.N. is in the Congo at our request; that means that it is to help us—not the other way round. That was the Belgian colonial way—but it is not possible today.' This speech was received with the most enthusiastic applause by all the Congolese; the U.N. representatives, Dayal and Linner, remained subdued.

Another and less serious occasion on which we were present at an official dinner in the President's house was when Mennen Williams, an American Assistant Secretary of State, visited Léopoldville. On that occasion the speech of Mennen Williams, in the Congo for perhaps forty-eight hours, caused some raised eyebrows among the Congolese when he announced that the Congolese man and woman whom he had met in the street had told him about independence; and how he fully understood what the Congolese and others in Africa had been through and suffered because the Americans had had just the same experiences themselves. It happened to be a moment when Rhodesia, with Roy Welensky—its Prime Minister—as spokesman, was pressing for its own independence. I could not help, maliciously I fear, saying to an American fellow-guest that, with Rhodesia much in the news at the time, the remarks of Mr. Mennen Williams would be interpreted as equating Roy Welensky with George Washington. And what, I asked, had happened to the Red Indians in the United States?

Life was not always dominated by serious affairs of state even in those days of late summer. We decided to celebrate Nigerian Independence on 1 October by inviting to a party all the Nigerians (mostly small traders) in Léopoldville, about eighty so far as we could find out, including their families. The time was fixed for 6–8 p.m. and, as the weather was dry, we made our arrangements in the garden. No one quite knew how such a party might go; but we had heard tales that it was the habit of these Nigerian families to bring paper bags which the children filled up with eatables when they had consumed what they wanted on the spot. We therefore laid on not only many cases of soft drinks but prepared some 2,500 items of food ranging from small sandwiches to substantial hunks of bread and masses of sticky cream buns. As it neared 6 o'clock the guests began to arrive on foot and by taxi. Exactly at 6 o'clock there were distant sounds of music rapidly drawing nearer; and in a minute two buses had drawn up full of Nigerian men, women, and children, and complete with a four-piece band playing lustily. They had come from Brazzaville across the river as they had heard that there was to be a party at our house and wanted to join in. This swelled our numbers to some two hundred in all and the newcomers took over the party. At once a ring was formed on the grass, the band struck up and played without ceasing for two hours. The women danced, slow rhythmic circling; and if a man particularly admired the dancing of any individual, he would go up to her and give her a coin. My wife joined in for a time and was extremely pleased to be given the equivalent of sixpence by an unknown admirer. Her pleasure, however, was ruined when she handed the coin to me to keep in my pocket and I handed it over to an old lady who, without exciting my admiration for her dancing, came up to me and demanded to be given a reward. The food went, steadily and rapidly, and soon the paper bags were being filled. Because we had so many more guests than we had reckoned on, all the food disappeared before the party was half over. In an effort to compensate for this, I brought out a number of bottles of whisky to add to the soft drinks. In due course, but still well before the end, our head servant came up to me, with impassive face, and said that we would need more whisky as it was nearly finished. This seemed hardly credible when a maximum of perhaps fifty adult males were present and the women and children and young people were strictly teetotal. The briefest watch on the bar gave the answer. The customers were a stream of small boys on behalf of their fathers. They took the proffered glass with a peg of whisky but declined any soda or water or ice. They hopped across the lawn to father who tipped the liquid into a bottle in his pocket and sent the boy back for another peg. This I thought was going too far and I did not produce any more. The party ended therefore with food and drink completely finished some time earlier. That, however, did not seem to matter nor had the slightest effect on the general gaiety. Promptly at 8 p.m. the head of all the Nigerians led the departure and by 8.10 no guests remained, after one of the happiest and most enjoyable parties we have ever given.

The only other large outdoor party we gave that summer had been before Independence on the occasion of the Queen's official birthday, in June. Again, about the same number of people were present, but mainly British on this occasion. In order to liven the proceedings we had obtained the services of the Salvation Army Band, quite a good musical ensemble under a young British Salvation Army officer who with his wife ran a school in the middle of the African city. From a discussion with him, some days before the event, of the programme of music which his band would play, it appeared that Salvation Army bands were only allowed to play hymn tunes. As we tried to picture our guests drinking whisky to the strains of 'The Church's One Foundation', their leader explained with a smile, 'Many of our hymn tunes are songs like "Poor Old Joe" and we can swing them.' They duly came and played and the party began to the strains, easily recognizable, of that well-known Salvation Army hymn 'We are drifting to our doom'. This greatly amused Elwyn Jones who happened to be staying with us that day and who said that he would watch anxiously after Independence to see whether this forecast proved true. With the Congo river flowing fast and wide in front of our garden, it did indeed seem an inapt moment for the tune. It was an overcast evening and we needed the lights with which we had decorated our garden. The Governor-General arrived just as the lights fused; and thereupon the D.D.T.-spraying tractor came round the roads on both sides of our garden, emitting its usual immense billowing clouds of disinfectant across it (this was a weekly health measure of the municipality in all the residential areas of Léopoldville). Just then, too, a fine drizzle began; and the band, with more sense of occasion than I am sure they realized, struck up 'There's no place like home.'

8

A particularly unfortunate event was the affair of the Ghana representative on 21 November. This was a direct result of the lack of any real contact between the U.N. and the Congolese government, and of the refusal of the U.N. to accept fully the fact that General Mobutu and his Commissioners were the government of the Congo for the time being, and that they therefore had to do business with them. Djin, the first Ghana Ambassador, had been replaced by Welbeck, who was now declared *persona non grata* by the Congolese and ordered to leave the country. He refused to move out of his house, presumably on the instructions of Nkrumah, with whom he was in direct touch through a communications detachment of the Ghana forces. After the expiry of his time limit he was given a further ultimatum which he declared himself unwilling to accept. The Congolese thereupon took steps to expel him by force, in the first instance from the house in which he was living.

This house was protected, unlike the residence of any ambassador, by a U.N. guard consisting of a picket of Ghana police. Welbeck had asked the U.N. to strengthen this protection and to help him in asserting his right to stay. This was a request which should not have been entertained; he was a personal representative of Nkrumah, not even an accredited ambassador. All through one afternoon the crisis built up; everyone knew what was happening and that a showdown was imminent. We had a visitor from London on that day and, as my wife and I walked him in the evening round the part of the city and along the river front near us (we lived about two-thirds of a mile from the Ghana Embassy), the streets were unusually empty. One or two lorries of troops passed us—U.N. troops on the way to reinforce the guard on the Ghana Embassy—and we saw a detachment of Congolese troops moving up to carry out the expulsion order. Soon after we got back from our walk the shooting began—desultory and isolated shots at first, building up from time to time in a crescendo of gunfire. Troops had arrived outside the house and the Congolese colonel in charge went in to escort Welbeck out. The colonel was at once shot dead by a Ghana security guard. With intermittent pauses the shooting went on for most of the night; thousands of rounds must have been fired. Welbeck went in the morning, leaving behind an intense bitterness among the Congolese who had lost half a dozen killed including the lieutenant-colonel, a deepened estrangement between the U.N. and the Congolese authorities, and a general resentment and hatred against Nkrumah.

This futile and unnecessary occurrence would have been avoided if the U.N. had refused to support Welbeck and had withdrawn its protective picket instead of reinforcing it. Nothing untoward would have happened to Welbeck personally; but it would of course have been a loss of face—once his original attitude had been declared—both for him personally and for Nkrumah. It was unfortunate that at that particular time Dayal, the permanent head of the U.N. Organization in the Congo, was in New York for consultations and that the Indian Brigadier Rikhye, Hammarskjøld's military adviser, then temporarily in the Congo, was acting in his place: von Horn was ill (he finally left the Congo on 12 December). The situation in the Congo was not such that a soldier, however well trained, could reasonably be expected, in a brief visit to the Congo, to have made the necessary contacts and acquired sufficient insight to take political control of the U.N. operation. I have no doubt that Rikhye may have been in wireless communication with U.N. Headquarters in New York during the day and received instructions on his course of action. But that is not the same thing as keeping in touch with a rapidly evolving situation on the spot and having the authority to make what was obviously the sensible decision—namely not to assist Welbeck to remain in the Congo against the wishes of the Congolese. It was no part of the U.N.'s mandate to do this. Furthermore, during that same day Major-General Alexander, Chief of Staff of the Ghana forces, had been sent by Nkrumah to Léopoldville with an order not to withdraw Welbeck unless absolutely necessary. Instead of taking him out at once, however, on his arrival at about 3 p.m., and telling the Congolese authorities that he was doing so, Alexander lost several valuable hours in trying to assess whether or not it really was necessary to take Welbeck away. It was only indeed when the situation had led on to fighting that he decided to do so; but by then, it was impossible (as he has described in his own book) for him and Rikhye to get near Welbeck's house during the hours of darkness, without crossing the lines of gunfire. Yet another complication was that Nkrumah wished immediately to replace Welbeck by another ambassador if he was indeed compelled to withdraw him; and he let it be known that he had no intention of seeking the agreement of the Congolese government to the appointment. This preliminary step is a necessary part of the appointment of any ambassador in any country—usually formal but occasionally resulting in a change of appointment, when the receiving government, for whatever reason, expresses reluctance to accept the person proposed. The Congolese, for their part, were adamant that no new ambassador would be accepted until his name had been submitted to them by Nkrumah in the usual way and their approval obtained. Until the arrival of the plane from Ghana in which Alexander travelled, it was generally believed that Nkrumah's insistence on sending the replacement would produce a further scene at the airport when the aircraft landed. However, whether or not the replacement was on the aircraft, this additional threat did not cause any further complication; no one stepped forward to claim the succession. This deplorable episode provided a damning indictment both of the handling of the U.N. operation and of the relations between the U.N. and the Congolese government; and of the misreading of the situation by the Ghana authorities. The next day I received a telegram from Ghana stating, 'Alexander convinced that but for U.N. protection Mobutu's troops would have killed the Ghana Embassy staff.' Nothing could have been further from the truth: the Ghana Embassy staff were in no danger from the Congolese until the battle began.

The Welbeck incident had immediate and disastrous consequences. The morning after the battle, some thirty-five cars with U.N. markings were stopped on the roads and either destroyed or taken away by enraged groups of Congolese (mainly troops). Members of the Ghana contingent, already unpopular, had to remove their badges in Léopoldville to avoid molestation. Ghanaian civilians long resident in Léopoldville also suffered. And the relations between the Congolese and the U.N. had deteriorated to a point where they could never be restored by those who were then in charge of the U.N.'s operations in the Congo.

During the crisis correspondents came from all over the world—from newspapers, news agencies, and radio and television networks. For a considerable period there was a daily U.N. press conference; but much could not be said when delicate situations were being dealt with. This sent the correspondents off on their own and many were the lurid stories which went off. Some of these were true; but not all the correspondents were seeking the truth, with the desire to present the picture in the round. At one time, for a period of some weeks, the Congolese Army had a picket stationed at the corner of our garden, to prevent Lumumba's escape from the encircling U.N. troops who guarded him fifty yards away. One day outside our house a newsreel cameraman came up and talked to one of the Congolese soldiers, then retreated down the road and drove up again at speed in his car, for the Congolese to stop him with levelled gun. The rehearsal was not good enough, so the episode was repeated with appropriate expressions of fierceness on the part of the Congolese and of daring courage by the camera team. A couple of days later this scene was on the television screens (perhaps I should not say of which European country) as an example of the hazards of life for the Congo correspondents. But it was not really so dangerous to be stopped with a tommy-gun through the window of the car. In all the crisis months I never knew of anyone being killed or even wounded in this way; though it was of course necessary to stop. Our own record was being stopped seven times on our way out to dinner and back—four times on the way out and three on the way back. I was driving—our driver went home to be with his own family at night—and on each occasion when we were stopped I said who I was and showed my pass. Sometimes the holder of the rifle was illiterate; but our conversation gave time for his N.C.O. to come up and then we were allowed on. It took all our self-control not to laugh in the face of one of the sentries when, having examined my pass (upside down), he announced that it showed that I came from Stanleyville—by then forbidden territory. 'No,' I replied, 'I really am the British Ambassador.' '*Tu mens*' was his rejoinder. It must be rare for Her Majesty's representative anywhere to be thus rudely told that he is lying; perhaps it was about the only French the soldier knew, from having heard his Belgian officer say it to him. At all events, my wife and I managed to hide our mirth at his remark and in a moment or two the sergeant came along and let us proceed to our dinner.

Some correspondents brought with them their prejudices and others acquired new ones to an extent which produced sometimes very distorted reports. I had some personal experience of this: in a leading British paper for example one Sunday four sentences appeared about me; three were wrong and the fourth had a false innuendo. And on another occasion a lengthy despatch contained half a dozen false statements attributed to me personally. In neither case was any attempt made to check with me the truth of the statements. Prejudices could be of various kinds—anti-Belgian, anti-'colonialist', anti-West, anti-East, anti-black, uncritically pro-U.N. actions in the Congo—this mostly in those who wished to stand well with African extremist opinion—and so on. It seemed surprising that serious papers should have continued to accept reports which failed to distinguish between fact and comment.

At one time it was suggested to me that I should have a regular meeting with half a dozen British correspondents to discuss with them the background of what was happening and to give them, in confidence, my views of the situation as it developed. I only had one such meeting. It was at a time of high tension between the U.N. and the Congolese and I spoke critically of U.N. attitudes and actions. One of the correspondents went round straight away to the U.N. staff at Headquarters, repeated what I had said of them, and asked what they thought of me. He thus got two stories, so to speak, for the price of one; but it forced me to change my intentions and to resume my practice of only being willing to discuss matters on an individual basis with journalists (whether British or not) whom I felt that I could trust. Such meetings were of course at least as useful to me as they may have been to the journalists concerned.

Much could be excused in all this because of the chaotic conditions of living and working which the situation imposed on the correspondents. It was indeed surprising how much good and careful reporting went out of the Congo and how some of the journalists kept going. They did not always manage to keep fit: one of the best went down with the only human case of foot and mouth disease which I have ever known.

Sometimes there were physical risks for them to run, beyond the normal for life in the Congo in those days. One night, when the regular ferry to Brazzaville did not run and the Léopoldville telex was not working, two correspondents wanted urgently to get their messages away. They went to a village just above Léopoldville and, after hard bargaining, hired a canoe with two paddlers to take them across the two-and-a-half miles of fast-flowing Congo river. Half way over, the paddlers stopped and demanded double pay. No protest availed and no explanation that the correspondents had no more money with them—there was little common language to carry on this sort of dialogue. There was less time, however, because the rapids began just below Léopoldville and no craft had ever survived them. The thought that if the correspondents themselves went over the rapids, so would the paddlers, was not altogether reassuring. Suppose the paddlers threw them out? So in the end the double fare was agreed; alas, only one correspondent got through from Brazzaville to London before his paper's last edition was run off: the other was too late.

A particular and charming friend of ours was Gabriel Makoso, the

Director and Editor of the daily *Courrier d'Afrique*. His paper had been supported by the Belgians but that did not deter him from freely criticizing Belgian policy when he felt it was needed. All through the most topsy-turvy times, he courageously wrote his leading articles with no regard to the consequences to himself; and more than once he was arrested, under successive post-Independence regimes, for making his contribution to the course of events.

It was not only some journalists who became emotionally involved in the Congo situation as it developed. More and more senior U.N. officials tended to forget the purpose for which they were in the Congo—to help the Congolese to find their feet—and tried to arrogate to themselves the power of forcing developments in the Congo into the channels which they, and not the Congolese, thought desirable. Basically, the Congo upheaval produced a situation in which the final outcome, if it was to be real and lasting, had to be the resultant of the various forces at work in the Congo—personal, tribal, regional, political, economic, and so on. It was the refusal of the U.N. to accept the limitation of their own role that led to the growing friction (which began within the first month of the U.N.'s presence in the time of Lumumba's government) with the Congolese, and ultimately to the unlamented final departure of the U.N. forces from the Congo. This friction need not have arisen: it did not with some of the specialized assistance which was given—notably the W.H.O. contribution. The Swedish General, von Horn, who was the first commander of the U.N. forces in the Congo, in his recent book *Soldiering for Peace* has described the chaotic ineffectiveness of the U.N. organization. His inside view corresponds with my outside one; and I could not better his description that the U.N. administration was filled with a passion for formalism, and manned by people who became a swarm of angry bees when their hive was threatened with criticism. When the head of the U.N. operations called the Congolese Army 'barbarians', it was hardly surprising that relations were difficult and strained with Mobutu, who was at that time head of the government. And when the U.N.'s attempted assumption of superiority and control of what was to happen in the Congo was challenged by the Congolese, scapegoats were looked for in order to justify the U.N.'s failure. Among these were the British government and, sometimes directly, myself, as their agent in the Congo. Thus the British were frequently accused of fomenting and supporting Tshombe's move for the independence of Katanga. This was a wholly false allegation: I should know, because I would have been the person through whom the support was conveyed. The fact that our consistent advice to Tshombe was against making any attempt to secede was disbelieved (or so they said) by those whose policy it suited to attack the British government at that time. U.N. policy, if it could be called a policy, was that Tshombe was a bad thing and everything had to be done to suppress him. Some catastrophic things were done, the last (in September 1961) bringing Hammarskjøld hot-foot to the Congo to find out for himself what was going on in his name, and leading him to his tragic end. What reports went to U.N. Headquarters in New York from Léopoldville I do not know—from the results that ensued, I can only assume that they were neither complete nor balanced; and indeed in that winter of 1960–61, two senior and very well-placed officials of the U.N. in Léopoldville (neither of them British and one an African) sought me out, separately and privately and at an interval of some weeks, to tell me that U.N. reports, officially compiled for Hammarskjøld, were being doctored before despatch so as to present a picture of events which was not according to the information available to the U.N. but which suited the then policy of the Afro-Asian bloc extremists. I reported these approaches to London at the time. The intemperate abuse of Britain when Hammarskjøld died, including the allegation by Nkrumah that the British had caused his death, was only one example of the intensity of some nationalist leaders' fervour with which the U.N.'s conduct of its Congo operation was continually bedevilled.

It was in small things as in big that this showed itself. One evening an English secretary, working at the U.N. Headquarters in Léopoldville, went out with a Sudanese officer. Unfortunately for them, they motored after dark near a Congolese Army camp on the outskirts of the city; their car was stopped and the Sudanese officer roughly handled. The girl took refuge for the night with an English resident who lived near by and who brought her in the next morning to the U.N. offices, where he dropped her to go in and do her day's work. The Sudanese officer had by then made his report, and at once the U.N. Headquarters released a story that this English girl had been raped by Congolese soldiers. This story went on to the ticker machines and by afternoon queries were coming back from London. In fact, when I had first heard the story, I had checked with the British resident in whose house she had stayed the night and who reported that nothing in the girl's behaviour led him to suspect that she had been raped. I sent our Consul round to see her at lunchtime, when he found her having a drink with some friends. She declined an offer to have a passage back to England arranged for her, or even to see a doctor. A subsequent protracted U.N. inquiry found that the rape story was untrue. And it happened a couple of years later that in a remote area of the Sudan my wife and I met again the Sudanese officer concerned, and heard a first-hand account of the story. There had never been any question of rape. I came to the conclusion that the reason why the U.N. had been in such a hurry to put out this sensational but untrue piece of news was because they were anxious at that time to prove how undisciplined the Congolese soldiery were and so how necessary it was for the U.N. to suppress the power of the Congolese Army and Mobutu. And the rape of a British girl by Congolese soldiers would have been good supporting evidence.

Dayal had arrived in the Congo on 8 September 1960 as the Secretary-General's special representative to take charge of the U.N. operations. He could hardly have arrived at a worse moment: the whole situation had changed in the previous two days. It soon became clear that Lumumba remained for him the Prime Minister of the Congo; and he adopted a contemptuous attitude towards Mobutu and the Commissioners. This attitude was embodied in the recommendations of his report to Hammarskjøld at the beginning of November; and this report, as General von Horn has remarked, effectively wrote finis to Dayal's work in the Congo. It made the Congolese feel—those who had the power at the centre—that there was no help to be had from the U.N. under its existing leadership in the Congo backed by the advice of the Afro-Asian extremists in New York. The Congo had to find its own salvation, in tragically many ways, despite the U.N. rather than with its help.

Stanleyville provided a good example of how the principle that U.N. forces were not to 'intervene in or be used to influence the outcome of any internal conflict, constitutional or otherwise' worked out in practice. Over two thousand Ethiopian troops stayed passive in the autumn of 1960 not only while those exercising power in Stanleyville ousted, degraded, and imprisoned the local provincial government of Orientale province, but also while a succession of hideous brutalities was perpetrated in Gizenga's name (he claimed to lead the legal government of the Congo) on great numbers of the inhabitants of that city and province. Gizenga's administration also arrested, imprisoned, and maltreated— one lost an eye—a group of Lumumbist members of the central legislature when they arrived in Stanleyville to explain to their electors why they no longer supported Lumumba. The protection of these legally elected representatives was specifically enjoined on the U.N. by the terms of one of the Security Council Resolutions. The world heard sometimes of the excesses committed against Europeans: no one heard or cared about the tortures and killings inflicted on many times the number of fellow Africans. Few outside the Congo knew, for example, that many Congolese in Stanleyville were tied hand and foot and thrown into the Congo river, or of the many other excesses committed by the indisciplined soldiers and civilian bands on whom Gizenga chiefly relied for his position.

The role of the U.N. forces in the face of these occurrences was sometimes repulsive. A particular example of the sort of thing which went on occurred on 27 November. On that day at about 6 a.m. all the Europeans in Stanleyville were awakened and dragged or driven (some in pyjamas) into army trucks. Some were taken to the District Commissioner's office and others put under arrest in the military camp where a stream of soldiers visited them, shouted abuse, ordered them to kneel or squat, and sometimes butted them with their rifles or cuffed them. Several Belgians were severely beaten up and women and children got the same treatment; no distinction was made for those Belgians—such as four school-teachers—who had returned to Stanleyville at the special entreaty of the provincial government. The official reason for the round-up was to check documents and put a new stamp on them. This stamping was done after some delay by the District Commissioner with the Minister of the Interior looking on. A crowd of about forty hysterical Congolese hustled each person in, distributing blows on the way and occasionally forcing the victim to run the gauntlet of their rifle-butts in the street. Many remained in the sun without even water from 7 a.m. until 5 p.m., and others were thrust into a small room which soon held seventy men, women, and children who were not allowed to leave it for many hours. Throughout the day Congolese soldiers went about threatening and beating. The Minister's own special Belgian adviser, who had returned at the Minister's special request a fortnight earlier, was severely beaten up in the Minister's presence. By the end of the day thirteen Belgians were in jail, illegally detained for real or imaginary irregularities of their documents. The French Vice-Consul, who had done his best all day to protect the Belgians from violence, obtained an assurance from the District Commissioner that these prisoners would not be beaten; but this promise was broken during the night and the following days. During all this time the U.N. troops never once intervened to protest or protect anyone; indeed the U.N. report for the day to Léopoldville Headquarters described what had gone on as a 'routine check of documents'.

Similar scenes went on at the airport where a woman member of my staff, who happened to arrive in Stanleyville that very morning, was beaten, insulted, and searched—diplomatic immunity meant nothing in the conditions of Stanleyville at that time. Then too a number of Ethiopian troops stood by placidly while she and others were dealt with in this way. They only galvanized themselves into action to take charge of a U.N. civilian official who arrived at the airport.

A sense of utter insecurity was widespread, not only among the Europeans: the staffs of Unilever and British-American Tobacco Co., for example, had many dangerous and unpleasant experiences. Many of the Congolese employees, too, of the tobacco factory were severely beaten up; and it became obvious that the factory would have to close sooner or later. The next day there were seven hundred Congolese prisoners being kept all day in the sun in a small open courtyard; and similar occurrences were taking place elsewhere. A great deal of this could have been averted if the U.N. troops had asserted themselves instead of showing utter inertia and a reluctance to take any action; it was due above all, however, to the lack of any orders from the U.N. Headquarters in Léopoldville about what they should do.

The refusal of the U.N. to recognize a change of government brought about by a military coup was a serious development in a rapidly altering situation. Presumably on instructions from New York, Dayal took the line that the U.N. had been asked to come in and help by Lumumba and his government. While not actively opposing Mobutu and his Commissioners, the U.N. Headquarters continued therefore to behave as if Lumumba's government was still the legal one; and in pursuance of that dual policy, they gave tacit support and some financial help to Gizenga when he set himself up as Lumumba's true and legitimate successor claiming that he intended to carry on the legal government of the Congo from Stanleyville. In my time in the Congo relations between the central government and the U.N. shifted uneasily in one direction after another, and the problem of Katanga exacerbated all other problems. If the U.N. had been flexible enough to be able to adjust to changing circumstances, many things would have been different. But it was rigid and aloof in its dealings with the Congolese, and the gap of understanding widened. It became clear already by the early autumn that the high hopes with which everyone had greeted the U.N.'s arrival on the scene two months earlier were not going to be justified. No one had thought what to do if Lumumba disappeared from the scene.

Blame for this has to be shared between the U.N. Organization as such and the agents it used in the Congo. Formally, perhaps, the Security Council should have decided that Lumumba's appeal lapsed with the downfall of his government, and that a fresh request for assistance from the new government was required if the U.N. operation was to continue. But, in the circumstances prevailing in the Congo and in New York in the autumn of 1960, that sort of process was unthinkable. As a result, the original mandate remained formally operative; and in pursuance of it the U.N. withheld recognition from Mobutu. By keeping to a position of apparently impartial *de jure* non-recognition, the U.N. in fact helped to cause a great deal of unnecessary friction and trouble, and enabled a regime of force and brutality to continue for months in Stanleyville and Orientale province. A U.N. finance officer indeed boasted to me on one occasion of the fine impartiality with which he had done a rapid tour of Congolese provincial capitals distributing money to the governments he found—including Gizenga's at Stanleyville and an even more implausible one at Bukavu, capital of Kivu province.

The U.N.'s position on this matter of bestowing or withholding recognition as circumstances demanded worked, of course, in favour of rebels against the new government. So far as I know, the U.N. has had no problem in recognizing new governments, say in Ghana or Nigeria, which have taken over after violent revolution. Why, then, not recognize that in the Congo? To some extent this may have been due to the nature of the individuals concerned with decision-making in this matter; but also it is true that there was no precedent and there had been no discussion in the Security Council on this point when the original Resolution about the Congo had been passed. Apparent neutralism worked actively against the government in power in the capital; and this fact—that seeming impartiality was itself a positively weighted policy—was one cause of the strong feelings which the Congo situation produced in New York, and of the arguments which went on in the Congo itself all through that winter of 1960–61.

Over all the U.N.'s Congo involvement at this time brooded also the much wider question of a threat to the U.N. itself and to the position of the Secretary-General. That autumn was the time when Khrushchev produced his 'troika' proposals, and when Russian representatives made intemperate attacks not only on the Organization as such but on

Hammarskjøld personally. To defend the U.N. and himself it was clearly necessary for the Secretary-General to have the support of Afro-Asia with its many votes: such were the passions aroused by the Congo at that time that this could only mean a degree of acquiescence in the policies required for the Congo by Nehru and Nkrumah. Both were deeply concerned with the U.N. Congo operation and it is perhaps not too far-fetched to believe that the U.N.'s policy in the Congo had to be such as—to put it negatively—not to offend them to the point where their support of Hammarskjøld might have wavered in New York.

9

The young Commissioners who had taken over from Lumumba in September made a good start; and they included a number of competent young men. Apart from finding their work bedevilled by worsening relations with the U.N. (which of course neither had direct control over the administrative machine nor over the Congolese Army)—and thus working in an increasingly uneasy partnership with the U.N.— they faced the serious rebellion against their authority in Orientale province. Gizenga exercised from Stanleyville a control by terror over considerable areas. In Katanga Tshombe was hovering on the brink of a declaration of independence; and in Kasai, Kalonji had set up his so-called capital on the site of the diamond mines (which produce something like seventy-five per cent of the world's industrial diamonds). Even in Léopoldville province there were mutterings of discontent.

In late September and early October Lumumba had made one or two sorties from his official residence, returning, however, quickly to base. Each time this happened the U.N. troops increased their watch-fulness, and the Congolese, with an outer ring of their army, surrounded the U.N. troops with the intention, after a certain point in time, of arresting Lumumba the next time he emerged. The U.N. refused to allow Lumumba to be arrested in his residence. The ring of Congolese troops included two pickets in our garden. They were frequently changed and we were therefore always being challenged on returning to our house. We found the first phrase in our Lingala grammar very useful: it read, 'This is my house.' To break out of this impasse and his position of increasing weakness, Lumumba decided to join Gizenga in Stanleyville and from there, with the hoped-for support of a number of Afro-Asian countries and perhaps the U.N. as well, reassert his authority over the whole country. Accordingly on the night of 27/28 November, he left Léopoldville in a small car and managed to get some hundreds of miles on the way to Stanleyville.

The day following Lumumba's night escape from next door was in its way dramatic for us. We had a lunch party which one of the Commissioners attended, and when we emerged from the house about 3 p.m. and I was seeing our guests off, I found a Congolese Army tank

T.H.—8

ensconced in one corner of the garden. Another one drew up at the next corner. The Commissioner and I walked up to the tank crew and asked what this was about, only to be told that it was believed that Lumumba had escaped and the Army intended to force a way into the Prime Minister's house to verify this, using arms if necessary against the U.N. guard which was still entrenched all round it. As I had no desire to be caught in a cross-fire of this kind, I suggested to the Commissioner that he go to the U.N. Headquarters and find out whether in fact Lumumba had escaped or not. He did so, finding with some difficulty someone to speak to; but informed me by telephone that he had been unable to get a satisfactory answer. It was by then 4 o'clock and there were signs not only of more Congolese troops coming up but of U.N. reinforcements to the guard round the Prime Minister's house. All seemed set for a battlepiece round about us.

This was not at all to my liking. I telephoned to the U.N. Headquarters and said that this was not an acceptable situation: either the U.N. must officially and at once declare that Lumumba was still in the official Prime Minister's residence, guarded by their troops, or else they must admit that he had escaped (with or without the connivance of his U.N. guards—that was irrelevant at the moment) and then remove their troops and allow the Congolese Army to search the house. I added that this had to be done forthwith, if we were to avoid the stupidity of another Welbeck battle; and, for good measure, I said that I was reporting my conversation by immediate telegram to London so that there should be no doubt where responsibility lay if the U.N. failed to act. Within the hour the U.N. troops had gone, the Congolese had searched the house and found that indeed Lumumba was not there.

Then began a three-day man-hunt, during which tension and apprehension mounted in the capital. It was clear that he would make for Stanleyville to join Gizenga; and the Congolese Army took all possible steps to catch him. They succeeded some four hundred miles from Léopoldville, and he was brought back to the capital. He was taken straight to a military camp, outside the reach of the U.N. to interfere with the arrangements. But so persuasive were his powers of argument that it was not long before it became clear that if he remained in a camp of General Mobutu's troops, he would succeed in subverting enough of them either to enable him to escape again or even perhaps to organize a counter-coup against Mobutu and Kasavubu. He had to be sent away; and as far as possible, and to a place where his reputation and political skills could avail him as little as possible. Katanga was indicated; and suddenly and secretly decided upon. On 17 January 1961 he was accordingly sent there by special plane. He was sent, I believe, with an escort of Baluba soldiers—members of the same tribe (possibly in one or two cases they had been personally involved) against which Lumumba had ordered so savage an army attack a few months before. The aircraft was not long in the air before the escort began to attack and beat him. The furore reached such proportions that the captain of the aircraft was forced to come back into the passenger compartment and order the guard to keep in their seats, as they were endangering the safety of the aeroplane. On arrival at Élisabethville, it was noticed by observers that Lumumba had been injured, and that he was roughly handled on leaving the aeroplane. He was then taken under escort to a house on the outskirts of Élisabethville. If he was left after his arrival in the custody of the same guards who had accompanied him in the aircraft (and it is my guess that he was) I have little doubt that he was dead by the morning— to the intense embarrassment of the authorities in Katanga for whom his presence was as unwelcome as it was unexpected. Responsibilities of all concerned in this, from the moment of decision to send Lumumba to Katanga, will probably never be finally disentangled. The persons immediately involved were very few in number, and some at any rate are unlikely to give a full and true account of events. It was a month before news of his death was officially given out from Katanga; but rumours about it had been current almost from the day of his arrival in Élisabethville. The doctor who certified death was never willing to say anything afterwards beyond the fact that Lumumba was dead when he saw him; a hastily ploughed-up field near the house where he spent his first night would seem to indicate that he, along with two companions, met his death there and his remains were buried at once, possibly after being cut up.

Lumumba had faced formidable problems in the few summer weeks which proved to be all that he had; in the end they had overwhelmed him because he lacked the capacity to deal with them. The news of his death was received calmly throughout the Congo, except in Stanleyville, where his supporters had taken over power and were maintaining what they claimed to be the legitimate successor government. That meant in effect exercising irresponsible authority with the assistance of some of the local troops of the Congolese Army (themselves in an increasingly undisciplined state), Gizenga's new levies, with uniforms and arms brought from Egypt by a U.N. aircraft, and a kind of youth brigade under one of the more notorious young thugs whom the revolution had thrown up. In Stanleyville a memorial meeting was held, days of mourning decreed, and a square named after Lumumba. But in Léopoldville and over most of the rest of the Congo nobody paid the slightest attention; and the equestrian statue of King Léopold II continued to be floodlit every night in front of the Palais de la Nation (as indeed it continued to be until we left the Congo many months later). There was no sign of public mourning in the capital and no attempt to commemorate Lumumba in any way. The Congolese are realistic about death, for them a much less emotive occurrence than it is with many Europeans. And they had seen Lumumba in action at close enough quarters to realize that this was not one of the great leaders of Africa who had left them. It was astonishing to read day by day of the reactions in the rest of the world—the founding of Lumumba University in Moscow, the wild speeches of some African leaders, the debates in the U.N., and other manifestations of rage and hatred. Other political leaders have been murdered, in Africa and elsewhere, before and after Lumumba's death. But none of those events caused such a frenzied reaction. Why should this have been so?

A personal anecdote with a remote bearing on all this is perhaps relevant. When I was leaving the Sudan, in the spring of 1965, I paid a farewell call on the Ghana Ambassador in Khartoum, in accordance with the custom of departing ambassadors to pay a round of farewell visits to their colleagues. It was five days before we were due to leave; and very shortly after Nkrumah had sentenced to death the persons who had been accused, in a case which had gone on appeal before the Ghana Chief Justice, of being involved in a plot against him. The Chief Justice had acquitted the accused, and had then himself been dismissed by Nkrumah. I felt sufficiently strongly about this to make some very rude remarks to the Ambassador about the behaviour of his Head of State, ending up by saying (very undiplomatically, I am afraid) that I felt ashamed to be in the same Commonwealth as such a person. I then went on to add that, furthermore, I would like to give the Ambassador my opinion—and I had lived through that particular time in the Congo —that the greatest single cause of Lumumba's downfall (apart from Lumumba's own character) had been the poisonous advice which Nkrumah had poured into his ears. My call on the Ghana Ambassador was not prolonged; and he soon gave up any attempt to defend his Head of State. Within a minute of my departure, however, as the doyen of the Diplomatic Corps told me when I later called on him, the Ghana Ambassador telephoned to him and said that there was no custom in

Khartoum of all the other ambassadors making a presentation to a departing ambassador. He thought that this practice should be started, that the British Ambassador should be given such a present, and said that he was sending along his own cheque for ten pounds towards it. The Egyptian Ambassador (who was the doyen) circulated this proposal to all the other ambassadors. It was done in such a hurry, because of my imminent departure, that I too received a request for my views on this suggestion. I was forced to reply that I found this highly embarrassing because I would never be able to contribute to the leaving present of anyone else, and that in any case the suggested contribution was far too much. The proposal was, however, adopted, and on the day before my departure I was invited by the Egyptian Ambassador to a drink with him and all our colleagues, on which occasion I was presented with a very fine, large, and expensive inscribed silver tray— the only one, I believe, which was available for purchase at that time in Khartoum—engraved with the signatures of all my colleagues. I have not yet been able to fathom the motives of my Ghana colleague for an action which took place many months before Nkrumah fell.

Why, though, did Lumumba's death produce such a reaction in so many countries? It was, I think, for two reasons: the African extremists felt that they had lost one of their number (there, but for the grace of God, go I, was perhaps also a thought in their minds), and Nkrumah in particular perhaps thought that he had lost a disciple and one who might have brought one of the more important countries of Africa into his dream of empire. And secondly, because the regime which had succeeded Lumumba in the Congo was led by Kasavubu and Mobutu, men who were free from Lumumba's wild aberrations, stable in character, and secure in themselves. Both were Christians (a fact which, in itself, was perhaps an outrage to the communists and others); both dealt easily with Western friends; both mistrusted communist aims and the ambitions and motives of some of the more extreme African heads of state.

A French doctor had earlier written an interesting article on the personality of Lumumba and the political implications of his character. Describing Lumumba's activities after Independence, his frantic travelling, his incessant speech-making and hypnotic hold over his audiences, his foiling of non-existent plots, and so on, he summed up Lumumba as a perfect specimen of the paranoiac personality—the type of the fanatically aggressive reformer. The main points of this personality he listed as, first, hyperdevelopment of the ego; secondly, distrust of others: all who are not faithful are traitors; and thirdly, an inability to accept logic or unwelcome facts, or to conceive that he may be mistaken. This flamboyant, unbalanced, basically anti-social personality he saw, further, as the modern Central African personality, distorted and exaggerated. This 'African personality' was made up, he went on, of layers of beliefs superimposed on an archaic basis of custom and magic (the layers being, for instance, Christianity, Western ideas and wants, Marxism, Asiatic influences, etc.). Whereas a balanced modern African tries to harmonize and assimilate the layers, a paranoiac does not: any of them may respond to a situation. This accounted for the inconsistencies and violent changes in Lumumba's behaviour. In contrast, the writer saw the basic constituents of the 'African soul' as spirituality, dignity, faithfulness, and tolerance; and asked how Lumumba, who had none of these qualities, could so greatly influence so many Africans. He found the answer in fear. Since belief in supernatural forces in a hostile world is part of the basic layer of the African mind, fear of witchcraft and magic is almost universal. Lumumba's paranoia exactly fitted him for the role of a magic person; all plots against him fail, he triumphs alone against all odds, he seems invincible. To oppose him is therefore dangerous and may lead to the death or destruction of the opposer or his children. As long as such a man lived he would be feared, said the author, who ended with the prophetic remark, 'No doubt that his obsessive idea "I shall die for the people" will come true.'

This perceptive analysis explained the superstitious basis of Lumumba's influence over his countrymen—and he certainly was regarded by many as a supernatural being. It explains also the strength of his influence and, in a curious way, the absence of reaction to his death within the Congo. In Bantu thought the Cartesian axiom becomes 'I act, therefore I am'; but Bantu realism accepts that action and power end with death. It is true that in those parts of the Congo where Lumumba had the strongest following and where Gizenga was at the time in power, there were reactions to his death which took the form of violent attacks on missionaries and other Europeans; but these were in some places due to the disintegration and collapse of authority in areas where even in Belgian times primitive savagery had only just been held at bay. Lumumba also without doubt had great appeal for other 'layers' of thought among his countrymen: like Nasser for the Arabs, he was the hero and champion who made them feel strong by identification. He embodied, at that time and place, successful anti-colonialism. In this aspect he appealed especially to the young, less critical in judgement and more easily stirred by such an emotional appeal. Because of his rejection of tribalism as a basis for power, he appealed also to the detribalized urban intellectuals. There was no other leader in the Congo who had this power to anything like the same extent; it might have had immense influence if used with wisdom. He was the obvious choice for the Afro-Asian and Eastern powers to exploit with varying degrees of cynicism in their propaganda battles, and he appealed to those intellectual circles in the West who saw extremism as national aspirations which should receive their support. He was not a communist and indeed cannot be said to have held any consistent philosophy. He was an extremist only in his unscrupulous opportunism. He was willing to use communist help and would probably have been prepared to sell out to communism to some extent for his own ambitions, believing that he would be able to control the situation as it developed. Equally, I am sure that Nkrumah would have been disappointed in him in the end: he would have gone along with pan-Africanism only as far as it suited him.

Lumumba certainly had natural ability and a hypnotic power as an orator; he had also immense energy, limited personal courage, a kind of ingratiating charm, and a flair for dramatic action. But he was ruthless and callous about human suffering. His reverses of fortune were loudly blamed on the West; it seemed clear at the time, however, that it was his own fellow-countrymen who step by step turned away from the path along which he was leading them, repudiated his methods, removed his communist advisers and sympathizers from the scene, and finally killed him. Had he lived and continued his career, it is almost certain that the Congo would have received a very different constitutional structure; and his boundless ambition and energy would have added greatly to the problems of Africa. I suppose that I knew him about as well as any Western diplomat, and on various occasions at my table I brought him together (before Independence) with Congolese and Belgians of differing views so that perhaps private discussion could help to iron out differences which had already begun to seem alarming. To no avail however; I never heard Lumumba admit the possibility of any change from the road along which his consuming ambition was leading him. 'He is a no-good,' remarked Lord Dundee when we emerged from a fifteen-minute private interview with Lumumba on the day following the declaration of Independence. It was not that Lumumba was an evil person, but that the essential weakness of his personal character led him to adopt what seemed the easier expedients of the moment and took him rapidly to the slippery slope down which he plunged to his doom.

10

For long the dominating feature of the U.N.'s involvement in the Congo was the military. The number of troops rose to over twenty thousand from twenty-nine different countries, some of these being represented by only a very small number of individuals. For reasons of policy, it was decided at first that there should be no troops from the major powers and no white troops except Scandinavian. This was a serious barrier to the competent handling of the military situation. The command of troops of mixed nationalities is in peacetime a difficult exercise, requiring experienced commanders and staffs. This is the case even when the troops belong to countries with long military traditions. When, however, the majority of the troops in the Congo came from newly independent countries, in many cases had never been abroad before, and had officer cadres for whom greatly accelerated promotion had been the rule in the recent past, all the difficulties involved were not only increased but multiplied. And finally, in a moving situation of sometimes near-war, tension, and excitement, where every military action—or inaction—had political overtoyes, it is remarkable that the U.N. military effort had the limited degree of success which it achieved.

The presence of U.N. troops had a calming effect at some times and in some places; at other times and places there were irritating results. This was particularly the case, perhaps, with the Ghanaian and Egyptian troops, the former of whom received a constant flow of instructions direct from Nkrumah to a degree which made the life of their commanding officer more and more difficult. This fine soldier, Lieutenant-Colonel (later Brigadier) Michel, was so plagued by these orders that he was delighted (so he told me) to have his troops posted away from Léopoldville by the U.N. Command, despite instructions to him from Nkrumah that he should not leave the capital. He courageously replied to Nkrumah that he would take his orders from the U.N. command only, and to Nkrumah's chagrin obeyed his U.N. orders. The Egyptian forces were similarly in direct touch with Cairo whence they received both orders and supplies. Once the supply aircraft crashed in the Congo and was cordoned off, as soon as possible, by Egyptian troops who prevented the U.N. from investigating (in accordance with their orders) what the cargo had been. In fact, it was military supplies for Gizenga. And indeed at the time of Gizenga's bid for power in Stanleyville, the Egyptian battalion set up a communications section for Gizenga to keep contact with Cairo. This was no part of their duties as a U.N. contingent in the Congo and was performed in conditions of increasing difficulty and frustration for the members of the communications team.

The Swedish battalion, partly because it was thought that its members would not be able to stand the climate so well elsewhere and also because they would be the most acceptable to the Belgians in Katanga, was sent to Élisabethville. There, for so long as I was in the Congo, they had an easy time of it; and so attractive for them were the conditions of service with the blue berets that there was a waiting-list of volunteers: young men openly boasted that six months in the Congo would enable them to save enough money to pay their way through the university in Sweden.

One of the best battalions was the Malayan. Eight hundred men arrived (later increased to fourteen hundred), completely self-supporting, and with every officer a Malay. This was not the case with the troops from other parts of the Commonwealth such as Ghana and Nigeria, in each of whose battalions a number of British officers were also serving. What distinguished the Malay battalion, however, was not just their composition and obvious competence—they came from fighting the communists for a decade in the Malayan jungle—nor the impression they created soon after their arrival when they laid on an impressive military demonstration parade which I have never seen excelled anywhere; but, more important than all this, was their attitude to the Congolese themselves. One of the first things which they did, for example, was to hold an evening reception at their officers' mess, to which they invited General Mobutu and his wife as well as other Congolese officers. It was a pleasure to see the response which this evoked, and the instantaneous and obvious rapport which was thus set up within a very short time of their arrival. The Malays had as a cardinal principle of policy that they should make it quite clear that they had come to help the Congolese and wished to be friends with them; and of course it paid off handsomely. When they arrived, for example, at Coquilhatville, the capital of Équateur province, to relieve an earlier U.N. force, they found an unhappy relationship and a virtual boycott of the U.N. forces by the local people; this changed immediately when it became known that the Malay battalion had arrived. And many were the occasions on which one young Malay officer with a couple of scout cars turned up when an ugly situation had developed, perhaps at an airport when people were being arrested or threatened, and by the very courage and competence and the goodwill of their presence calmed the situation at once. I need hardly add that the Colonel and others of the battalion whom we had the pleasure of meeting could not have been more charming personally. It is wholly untrue that the Malayans 'regarded the Congolese as an inferior race sadly in need of being taught a salutary lesson', as von Horn apparently was told. It was just because this was not their attitude of mind that they were such a success.

An outstanding contribution to the calming of the situation in Léopoldville was made by the Nigerian police contingent of some 400 officers and men. The sight of unarmed and good-humoured policemen controlling crowds and traffic in the capital produced an immediate effect on the inhabitants; and many were the praises lavished on them. There had earlier been a Ghana police contingent which had also done well; but Nkrumah's policy made their continued presence impossible. The Nigerians were on occasion sent outside Léopoldville but in the main they stayed in the capital. Again, the secret of their success—apart from their discipline and competence—was the fact that they made it abundantly clear that they had come to help the Congolese in any way they could and took care to establish close and friendly personal relations with them. The Nigerian army command in the Congo also established close and good relations with Mobutu.

The Tunisian battalion made its mark as a loyal and efficient component of the U.N. force. Bitterly as they resented the role thrust upon them in the Welbeck incident (their comments on the U.N. direction which needlessly and wrongly involved them in this situation were unprintable), they continued unobtrusively to do their duty. Later they played a difficult part in helping to keep peace in the capital of Kasai province and as far outside as their limited means allowed.

Indian troops came into the Congo operation some time after the April 1961 upheaval and were stationed up-country—and Pakistan supplied several hundred men for supporting services. They also for the most part were outside Léopoldville. The troops from both these Commonwealth countries were of the quality which one would expect.

It was probably the case that no competent command could have been organized from the material provided and in the conditions prevailing both in the Congo and in New York at U.N. Headquarters. The unclear and changing directions of the U.N. efforts in the Congo were inevitably reflected in makeshift military arrangements. These led to numerous unpleasant incidents, from the serious to the merely funny: an example of the former followed from sending the Sudan's contingent to Matadi with inadequate preparation and liaison with the local Congolese; this led to the humiliating forced withdrawal of this fine company and to the Sudan's opting out of the whole Congo operation. One of the latter was provided when a Swiss officer came to organize Congolese Army training (again after no consultation with the Congolese Army authorities) and had to be evacuated from U.N. Headquarters in the middle of Léopoldville by helicopter three days later, in such a hurry that he left his luggage behind. This was because he could not begin to get his bearings in the Congo; anything more un-Swiss than the situation in the Congo in late 1960 would be hard to imagine.

However all that may be, and General von Horn's book gives an insider's view of the difficulties and frustrations of the military operations, the fact was that although a calming effect was produced by the presence of U.N. troops, the need for more positive kinds of military training and assistance and ways of achieving these were never either understood or, certainly, acted upon, because of the constant preoccupation of the U.N. Headquarters with trying to control political developments in the Congo.

Members of the U.N. Headquarters, however, maintained the minimum of contact with the Congolese. While driving herself about the town one day my wife met two members of the Pakistani U.N. forces whom we knew. One greeted her with the remark, 'Are you not afraid to drive yourself alone in Léopoldville?' Before she could reply, the other commented, 'Anyone can drive about Léopoldville alone except members of the U.N.'

Brzac, a Czech, who was the representative in Stanleyville of the U.N. in that province, said to me in mid-November 1960, when he was on a visit to Léopoldville, that the U.N. saw itself in the relationship of a parent to a small child: 'You do not let a child do what it likes,' he explained, 'or else it becomes destructive and grows up wrong. It needs to be told when and what to do, when to go to bed and so on.' This was fallacious reasoning: for good or ill, in the first week of July the world had given its approval to the coming-of-age of the Congo by admitting it to membership of the U.N. And, more importantly, the Congolese neither wished nor intended to allow themselves to be treated as children and put under a U.N. mandate. They were certainly uneducated and inexperienced, but they were neither children nor fools. One might indeed say that the brashness of the U.N. in making this its first venture, so to speak, in colonialism, caused acute problems which a different psychological approach would have avoided. In fact Brzac was being unfair to himself and was more enlightened in his deeds than in his exposition of the policy which he had to support; he achieved a certain success with two schemes of land and road development by his personal relationship with the Congolese concerned who came to trust him and seek his advice.

It was different however in Léopoldville where both the political and military chiefs of the U.N. failed in this respect. It was wholly unjustified publicly to denigrate the Commissioners, for example, by calling them 'students who have to call in their teachers to help them', when they were making use of the advice of academic economists; and unrealistic thereafter to expect that these young Congolese would wish to turn to the U.N. for help. Contrary to frequent references in the foreign press and radio, few of the twenty-nine Commissioners left university studies to take up office; most of them were in their late twenties and some in their thirties. Similarly, to call Mobutu 'a child' and his army 'a rabble' was not the way to encourage military co-operation with the U.N. As the U.N. had consistently snubbed the Army and given them no help except in the training of some parachutists (a wholly irrelevant exercise from the point of view of producing a disciplined army), it forced Mobutu to send his young cadets abroad for training. The head of the U.N. civilian operations returned a derisory reply to my suggestion that Mobutu should be consulted as to which officers, Belgian or otherwise, the Congolese Army should engage. It is small wonder that von Horn writes that the U.N. 'seemed doomed to exist in a perpetual aura of hatred'.

The malady however went deeper. For weeks at a time Dayal, the head of the U.N. Mission, never saw Kasavubu; and Dayal actually told my wife at a dinner one night that he had no time for Congolese visitors such as Mobutu and Bomboko who wanted to talk to him, because he had to get on with his work. The greater part of his work should have been to understand Congolese psychology, which is quite different from European or Indian, and that could not be done without much time spent in talking to Africans. Above all others Kasavubu embodied the Africanism and tribalism of the Congo; to try and understand what moved the Congolese and what kind of people they were, senior U.N. officers should have been in frequent conference and friendly meetings with Kasavubu and other leading Congolese. It was not as if they were a difficult people to know; on the contrary, they were easy and friendly to talk to, and willing to be talked with. The same story was repeated on the military front: when my Military Attaché suggested to a senior U.N. officer that U.N. officers should meet the Congolese more, the astonished reply was 'Do you mean to say that General von Horn should invite Mobutu to dinner?' This would have been amusing to hear if it had not been dangerous nonsense in the circumstances of the Congo in late 1960. Among other results, this lack of understanding and liaison produced the U.N. proposal which I have mentioned—to set up a training base for the Congolese Army, in the Congo, without any consultation with Mobutu. Mobutu rejected the idea when he heard of it, and nothing was ever done about it.

There was no possibility of getting away from this continuing friction and chaos, and from the hardening of positions on the part of both the U.N. and the Congolese, without a radically new psychological approach by the U.N. So long as it failed to make such a change, the U.N. was only maintaining a vast area of instability and unrest in the centre of Africa; or perhaps it would be fairer to say that the U.N. was postponing the day when the Congo would find its feet. So far were the U.N. leaders from understanding this that Linner, then the head of the technical operations, said to me once, when I was trying to persuade him that a new kind of approach was needed, that perhaps 'the colonialist powers were becoming jealous of the U.N.'s success in the Congo'. In this same conversation (in late 1960) this official expressed disapproval of the action of the Congolese President of OTRACO in bringing back Belgians to his organization, and disapproved also of the return, at the request of the Congolese, of twenty-eight out of the four hundred scientists who had been at the INEAC research station in Orientale province. His reasons for insisting on recruiting solely through the U.N. for this and other Congolese requirements were interesting. First, it would put the U.N. record straight, so that if Lumumba came back to power and asked the Russians to return, the U.N. could adopt the same policy towards them. To my inquiry whether he really thought that either Lumumba or the Russians would in that case pay the slightest attention to the U.N., he replied that he did not know. Secondly, he made much of the fact that some of the Belgian officials in the Congo were obstructing the carrying out of the U.N.'s work. I have already explained how I had recommended to Dayal to get over this particular hurdle; but I had failed, and the U.N.'s only solution was to keep all Belgians out of official or semi-official positions. Linner's third reason was that the Congolese were not competent to choose the Belgians they needed or wanted to return. This was in spite of the obvious fact that the quality of many U.N. technicians was poor—the Prime Minister of Kivu province, for example, complained that he could not use U.N. technicians who were sent to him because they knew nothing: he had had to turn to a local Belgian to repair the water system which a U.N. hygiene expert had been unable to do, and another of his U.N. team of engineers was a Swedish boy in his first year at university. The Congolese, on the other hand, who knew the Belgians, knew also exactly which Belgians they wanted back; and were fully competent to choose them.

It is necessary to go into this matter at some length and detail because it is basic to an understanding of the U.N.'s policy in the Congo and the limited nature of its success. When Dayal went, better relations were at once established with his successor; but by the end of 1960 the Congolese had come more and more to mistrust an organization which should have been the hope of a new country like theirs. It was dispiriting to hear the U.N. bitterly attacked by them and to listen to U.N. representatives being booed by the crowd as they drove away after the big Congolese Army parade on 17 November 1960. It must have been disquieting to Hammarskjøld that this should happen, especially when the individual Commissioners publicly stated the great benefits which the U.N. conferred on the Congo in certain specific fields—e.g. in helping to make arrangements for financial control, import licences, control over foreign exchange, and the like—and paid repeated tribute to the calming effect of the original arrival of the Ghana troops in the middle of July.

The final U.N. attempt at assuming the powers of a 'colonialist' was when it decided (without of course any agreement with the Congolese government and despite the opposition of the Congo representative in the U.N. Assembly meeting in New York) to hold an inquiry into Lumumba's death. A Resolution was adopted to this end on 15 April 1961, and was an extraordinary assumption of U.N. superiority. The U.N. had no more right to inquire into Lumumba's death than it would later have had to set up a commission to inquire into President Kennedy's death. Such are the rules of the game which the U.N. must follow and which it has no authority to transgress. The Commission which was appointed to make the inquiry was, not unnaturally, refused entry into the Congo; and nothing ever came of its report. The Congolese, although the Afro-Asian extremists would never admit it, were not *in statu pupillari* in respect of the U.N., and they had no intention of allowing themselves to be treated as anything other than a fully independent country, as entitled to look after its own affairs as any other, whether African or not.

To such a point did the U.N./Congolese relationship deteriorate that, so far as I knew, Dayal never saw Kasavubu from Christmas 1960 until the end of his term. He went back to New York in the early spring of 1961, and Mekki Abbas came to Léopoldville from the Sudan to act as head of the U.N. Mission during Dayal's absence: it was known that Dayal would be on a prolonged visit to New York. It so happened that on the day that Mekki Abbas was due to arrive I went to see Bomboko, the Foreign Minister, who was ill in hospital, and in the course of conversation said that I hoped he would take advantage of the arrival of a new head of the U.N. Mission to try and create a better working relationship between the Congolese government and the U.N. Headquarters in Léopoldville. To my surprise he said that he did not know of Mekki Abbas's arrival that day and explained this, with a smile, as being because 'as you know, we have no relations with the U.N.'. From the Foreign Minister of the country which the U.N. was so deeply committed to helping, this statement was revealing. It was a catastrophe that the world's desire to help the Congo should have been so frustrated by prejudice and incompetence in the dealings of the U.N. with the Congolese.

Mekki Abbas remained some ten weeks in the Congo, without knowing from one week to the next how long he would be there. He found it easy to create at once a good personal working relationship with the Congolese leaders, but he was himself hamstrung in taking any initiative as he never knew whether he would be there to see it through; nor did the Congolese, for their part, feel that they could rely on a new relationship with the U.N. because they did not know how long it would continue. This unsatisfactory position finally induced Mekki Abbas to ask to be relieved, shortly before Dayal was eventually due to return. The Congolese government refused to accept Dayal back and from Kasavubu downwards made it clear that they would take forcible measures, if necessary, to prevent his return. Accordingly, Linner, who had hitherto been in charge only of the technical assistance side of the U.N.'s activities in the Congo, was made acting head of the U.N. Mission, and Dayal's term was over.

I was sent to New York, from a conference which I attended in London in May 1961, to give Hammarskjøld a first-hand account of what was happening in the Congo. It may well be, since I believed it to be true and an important element in the situation, that I told him Dayal's return would be unacceptable to the Congolese. But the purpose of my journey to New York was not just to tell this to Hammarskjøld, as I have seen it stated.

I have also seen it suggested that Dayal's removal was part of a deal whereby the American Ambassador and I were also transferred from the Congo. Certainly so far as I was concerned this was not so. Apart from the fact that I do not believe that Hammarskjøld, any more than the British government, would have indulged in this kind of trafficking, I had some time earlier stated to the Foreign Office my wish not to do a second tour of duty in the Congo after my first was over at the end of July 1961. This request was readily and understandingly accepted. Not only was the work arduous—I do not think I had worked so hard since my last year at school—but the climate was not ideal. Although my wife and I kept in good health, this might well not have been the case with a further eighteen months; nor was it sensible to bring our children out to the Congo for their holidays. Moreover, the situation in the country was such, and seemed likely to continue in such a way, that it was undesirable for the British Embassy to be without an ambassador for as long a period as three months, which was the leave I looked forward to taking from August.

It is time to return briefly to Congolese political developments and to say a word on the series of conferences which were held in the first seven months of 1961 in order to try and work out a new constitutional structure for the Congo as a whole, and in particular to find a means of accommodating Katanga—and Tshombe as its spokesman—with the rest of the country. In accordance with the promise of Mobutu when he made his coup d'état in September, the College of Commissioners had come to an end early in 1961. This was after a round table conference in Léopoldville, called by Kasavubu. Not all the Congolese leaders supported the idea of a constitutional conference, notable absentees being Gizenga from Stanleyville and Tshombe from Élisabethville. The result of the conference, however, was to replace on 9 February the College of Commissioners by the government of politicians headed by Ileo as Prime Minister. At the end of the month, by which time Lumumba's death had been officially announced, Ileo went to Élisabethville and reached an agreement with Tshombe.

This meeting and agreement were facilitated by the many debates during February in the United Nations in New York when ideas on the future of the Congo were tossed about with complete disregard of the wishes of the Congolese. Needless to say, the Congolese government rejected the conclusions of these deliberations and, as a part consequence, drew together in a common front against the 'threat', as they saw it, of U.N. domination. It was agreed at the meeting in Élisabethville between Ileo and Tshombe that another conference should take place on neutral territory outside the Congo, so that no delegation would feel itself threatened. This was arranged to open in Tananarive in Madagascar on 8 March; and this time the conference was more representative than its predecessor in Léopoldville. In particular Tshombe attended, and so did the Prime Minister of Léopoldville province—a former supporter of Lumumba. But Gizenga and his allies in Stanleyville remained absent. The conference concerned itself mainly with the future structure of the state—such things as the number of provinces and the division of powers between the centre and the provinces. The Belgians had left the Congo divided into six provinces; as tribal feeling developed, more and more leaders demanded a province small enough to be controlled by their own tribe with themselves as the head of it; and the suggested number of provinces rose rapidly to the twenties.

A much better atmosphere reigned in Léopoldville after this Tananarive conference. Partly this was due to the change in leadership of the U.N. in the Congo, when not only did Mekki Abbas succeed Dayal for an important period of ten weeks, but two distinguished and able Africans, Robert Gardiner and Francis Nwokedi, became his chief assistants. These created such a feeling of personal trust that it was possible, with their active help, for the Congolese to arrange yet another conference. This one took place inside the Congo, at Coquilhatville, capital of Équateur province. It opened on 24 April and lasted four weeks. It was concerned with the implementation of the decisions of the Tananarive conference of the previous month, and came nearer to full participation by everyone concerned. Despite Gardiner's best efforts, however, Gizenga refused to attend, although he did send representatives. It early became apparent that widely differing views were held about what had been decided at Tananarive, and Tshombe walked out of the conference intending to return to Élisabethville. This was prevented by force and he was kept under house arrest at Coquilhatville while the conference went on; he was then brought to Léopoldville and detained in an army camp. This did not last long and he was released by Mobutu on the promise of sending a full delegation from

T.H.—9

Katanga to a further conference arranged for late July in Léopold-ville.

At this stage the U.N. did make a valuable intervention in the political stalemate. Mekki Abbas, with the assistance of Gardiner and Nwokedi, put in hand steps to facilitate the holding of the conference, with pro-tection of the participants guaranteed and carried out by U.N. forces. The conference was finally held in Lovanium University on the out-skirts of the capital in July 1961. From it emerged Cyrille Adoula as the Prime Minister of the Congo: this was a most promising development. In our last days in Léopoldville we invited Adoula to meet a prominent visiting Nigerian politician and they spent a long evening together in our house discussing the problems of government and what lessons Nigeria had for the Congo. Adoula was a mature Congolese, brought up as a trade unionist and with considerable strength of character and persona-lity; for him and his wife, who was a teacher, my wife and I had much respect and liking.

Tshombe, in fact, had gone back on his word and failed to send a delegation to the Lovanium conference at its opening. He came to Brazzaville, across the river from Léopoldville, soon after the con-ference opened. The chance which this offered to have informal dis-cussions with him was not seized, however. The uneasy relationship between Léopoldville and Élisabethville continued therefore all the time that I remained in the Congo; and by the end of July, when I left, another kind of attempt to settle it by force, this time by the U.N., was being prepared. Tshombe had, ever since the mutiny a year earlier, stiffened his forces in Katanga with European mercenaries, recruited mainly in South Africa but including also a number of British. This was an additional affront to the U.N.; and following a U.N. Resolution for the expulsion of mercenaries, we took over the passports of such British as we could get hold of, and sent the men out of the country. Most of the mercenaries were expelled in this way, though one or two found their way back again. The Katanga story was unfinished and the Congo's constitutional crisis not resolved when I left.

Two comments may perhaps be made on this sequence of events, which are necessary for any understanding of the Congo situation at this time. An African palaver is a long-drawn-out affair; it is necessary not to lose patience as the U.N. did, with an apparently endless succes-sion of meetings and conferences. This is the way the Congolese work; and it is a good way too. It gives time for the basic realities of a situation to overcome the temporary irrelevancies. Secondly, the Congolese leaders were wrestling with difficult problems which would have taxed the capacity of many more mature peoples. I knew many of the leaders, some of them well. Many were honestly trying to find an answer, and it would be a foolish person who would claim that a group of his own political leaders could have achieved quick results in dealing with such intractable problems. Seen from the worm's eye view of one living in the Congo at this time, the lengthy debates and resolutions of the U.N. might many of them have been about conditions on Mars for all the relevance they had to the situation in the Congo or for any effect they had on the evolution of the Congo's problems. The help of the U.N. was very welcome when it came from friendly, helpful hands and understanding minds. All too rarely, although notably from the three Africans mentioned above—a Sudanese, a Ghanaian, and a Nigerian— did the Congolese get what they wanted and so desperately needed.

II

I have criticized the manner of the U.N.'s activities. It is necessary, to put this great operation in perspective, to give some account of what it achieved despite its method of going about things.

First and perhaps most dramatic was the calming effect of the military presence, spotlighted by the arrival in Léopoldville in early July 1960 of two platoons of Ghana soldiers. Not only did these disciplined and well-led men show the disintegrating Congolese Army what they lacked; but the sight of a junior British officer saluting and taking orders from a Ghanaian, senior to him, was a revelation to the Congolese. The result was immediately to reduce, though not entirely to eliminate, the jitteriness at the possibility of the Belgians coming back. As more U.N. troops arrived and spread out over the country, this steadying influence spread, with varying degrees of effectiveness according to the relations established between the local U.N. and Congolese Army commanders. Conflicting orders to the U.N. forces, however, about the kind of neutrality which they were to observe soon unfortunately began to undermine their moral position and their effectiveness. Incidents like the beating up of Kasavubu's private secretary, a fine young Congolese, outside the U.N. Headquarters in the middle of Léopoldville, with dozens of U.N. personnel looking on, were destructive of confidence and morale on both sides. An example on the grand scale of the difficulties of preserving the U.N.'s special interpretation of neutrality occurred much later, when the U.N. decreed a neutral zone in North Katanga: then, when Lumumbist troops from Stanleyville penetrated through this zone, the U.N., having failed to prevent that, refused (by threat of the use of force) to allow Tshombe to expel those invaders himself from the province of which he was then the legitimate provincial Prime Minister. In between these occasions and all over the country, the conflicting orders from U.N. Headquarters in Léopoldville—perhaps a reflection of incompatible Resolutions in the U.N. in New York—steadily detracted from the value of the U.N. military presence. And of course all the time Mobutu was slowly but surely increasing his control over the Congolese Army. The presence of an enormous U.N. force, good, bad, and indifferent as its constituent units were, had a continuously dampening effect on outbreaks of violence throughout the Congo, and helped to give the country time to get its breath again. But you cannot, after all, help to keep order if you cannot decide which is the legitimate government which you ought to be helping to keep order.

Secondly, the U.N. technical assistance: here some most valuable work was done, dependent again on the relations set up with the different Congolese governments, departments, and authorities. Particularly valuable was the help given in matters of financial and monetary control, for which an excellent working relationship was established with the Congolese; and in the field of health, much was achieved. During the first year of independence, much useful technical assistance was given—from measures to ward off famine in South Kasai (the result of the Baluba-Lulua fighting) to help in running airports. General Wheeler, famous for clearing the Suez Canal after 1956, was invited to get Matadi port functioning again; and eight major surveys were started in the Ministry of Finance alone. Linner, who came to the Congo to take charge of this side of the U.N.'s work, set up an ambitious programme—with Lumumba's full support—and installed what could almost be called a shadow cabinet of his representatives sitting in with the Congolese in eleven of the principal departments of government. A public services commission was set up and an analysis begun of the future structure and requirements of various departments, and many other plans were made. It was obvious that there was going to be a U.N. technical assistance presence in the Congo for many years.

By the end of September 1960, the technical assistance programme was employing some 150 foreign consultants and technical advisers; and four special representatives had been established in provincial capitals to provide liaison with provincial governments and co-ordinate the work of U.N. teams. Plans were made at this time too for a massive programme of public works to help provide work for the rapidly increasing number of unemployed. Ambitious plans for educational development had to be drastically curtailed; but much help was given here also, and a number of countries, notably the United States, France, Germany, and Israel, took large numbers of Congolese students to train. The U.N. both set up special institutions (e.g. for agricultural training) in the Congo and assisted Congolese to go abroad. By the time I left the Congo some three thousand Congolese were following various courses outside the country. A useful beginning had therefore been made, but it was clearly going to be years before the Congo could catch up on the advanced training which the Belgians had denied them the opportunity of acquiring.

In a press conference in Léopoldville in late 1960, Linner emphasized that the U.N. could never allow itself to by-pass the Congolese government 'whatever government that may be'. This was the Achilles heel of the whole U.N. programme. If that principle had indeed been adopted, the story would have been different. But 'whatever government that might be' was interpreted by the powers above Linner as Lumumba's and, later, the Gizenga regime in Stanleyville which claimed to be the heirs of Lumumba's power. This political decision—highlighted through the months by the U.N.'s refusal to allow the arrest of Lumumba, followed by the forceful freeing from arrest in Léopoldville of Gizenga by the U.N. General Kettani personally, and Gizenga's subsequent protection by the U.N. forces in Stanleyville until he could establish himself there, the tacit acceptance by the U.N. of the recognition of Gizenga's regime in Stanleyville by various Afro-Asian powers as well as of material support from some of them for this regime, the emotionalism on the question of the return of Belgians to the Congo, and all the handling of the Katanga question, above all the cold-shouldering and denigration of Mobutu and the Congolese in power in Léopoldville—all this destroyed the chances of Linner's schemes coming to full fruition. Much was achieved, but much of the U.N. technical assistance effort was frustrated by these political developments which ought not to have occurred.

British official policy on the need for the U.N. to dispose of armed forces in 'an effective peace-keeping capacity'—to quote a recent Secretary of State for Foreign Affairs—supports the ideas that (i) governments should earmark contingents for a U.N. force; (ii) there should be a common military doctrine so that those designated forces can work together; (iii) there should be a planning organization in New York; and (iv) more countries should come forward with voluntary financial contributions.

From my experience and witness of the U.N.'s military operations in the Congo, I do not believe that any one of these four desiderata is sufficient in itself or precise enough. All four together leave us effectively where we are. Maybe general principles need statement; but the years pass and unexceptionable principles easily slide over into accepted clichés. Subject always to the proviso that history never repeats itself exactly, and that there will never be another Congo (there may be worse situations, but the conditions will not be the same), or even another Gaza Strip with all its particular overtones, I wish to offer some comments on each of these four proposals; it is not that I disagree with them so much as that I think they are void for insufficiency.

First, the earmarking of contingents: in and between the leading military powers it is possible theoretically to contemplate that this could be done and the forces incorporated in an overall plan; and, even though rapid and major changes are taking place in the composition and equipment of forces, to be certain that this commitment would not be lost sight of. But, except in a very few countries, it could not be seriously expected that an earmarked contingent would always be available for U.N. purposes, irrespective of national circumstances at the time or the extent of national interests involved in the situation then being dealt with by the U.N.; and, after all, the big powers have national interests all over the world. Is it expected that the earmarking of national forces would be so arranged that the forces available, and their equipment, would complement each other so that a complete and balanced force would result? If not (if the earmarking were left to each country, which would be most likely to nominate a contingent that it could most easily spare) or if some country or countries went back on their previous offer, then that particular force might be totally useless at a critical moment. The U.N. would be suddenly faced with the need to cut its coat according to its cloth and would, in my opinion, most probably find itself compelled to cut another kind of garment altogether because the material it could dispose of was the wrong length, perhaps too short, and the wrong quality, perhaps too thin. It would be unable, in fact, to take the necessary action. This would be more likely to happen the more important the occasion, and would be aggravated if the U.N. followed the principle adopted in the Congo of not calling on the major military powers to make force contributions. If that sort of thing is not to happen, how is the balanced nature of the force to be established? To plan the organization of such a force and to supervise its creation and ensure its serviceability require a major military headquarters associated with the United Nations. That sort of task cannot, in the nature of things, be done by middle-rank officers from under-developed or even neutralist countries.

Secondly, one thing which the Congo operation did demonstrate was how much easier it was for contingents who spoke the same language to operate together—I do not just mean the English language, though this was of enormous advantage where it applied—but who had the same ideas of staff work and training and military duties, and the right relationship of military forces and civilian control. The easy interchange which all this facilitated and encouraged in the Congo among the many Commonwealth contingents and at many levels, was constantly apparent and of obvious value. It could be so because the military links were, at that time, still one of the strongest working relationships in the Commonwealth. Both Nigeria and Ghana, for example, had British generals as their Chiefs of Staff and many British officers in their forces; and Indian and Pakistani troops had a common background which was still important and valuable. Much of all this has changed already; and most of it will inevitably be gone within a decade, when personal relationships will be much more attenuated and separate national developments increasingly in evidence. I can see no means of halting or even seriously delaying such a process so far as the Commonwealth is concerned, and no possibility of contemplating the introduction of common staff training for countries outside the Commonwealth. National rivalries, jealousies, suspicions, and the like are too strong, even if the mechanics of working out a common military doctrine were practicable, which in itself would require a high-level combined staff continuously at work.

If this is true, a modest central planning organization in New York would find itself trying to deal with such a variety of disparate considerations that it is hard to see how any sensible and workable plan could emerge—a plan not only for mobilization but for operations and for effective liaison with different countries as well as the U.N. political headquarters itself. At the time of the Congo operations, the Secretary-General of the U.N. had a Military Adviser (an Indian brigadier) with virtually no staff. It was an impossible arrangement to control a vast military involvement, thousands of miles away. This implies, I need hardly add, no criticism of the military competence of Brigadier Rikhye personally, a charming Indian Army officer. But it is hard to see how even an expanded Military Adviser's staff or a hastily created operational headquarters in New York could work out plans to meet changing situations, when it could not be sure that all the elements needed to work its machine would be available at the crucial moment. That is not an assignment that would attract the world's leading military men; and that is what is needed. A localized and isolated (from the military point of view) situation like the Congo demanded the skills, patience, and insight of one of the world's top generals to command the forces; in a more involved situation anything less would merely add a new dimension to the dangers which already existed. It is not much good having to improvise at the last minute: without a continuous flow of intelligence and information no sensible and effective planning is possible.

Lastly, the voluntary contributions: there are many objections to the way in which the U.N. operation in the Congo was financed; and it is surely unlikely that that method will be deliberately repeated. It is unfair to the idealistic nations to expect them to foot such bills—after all, every government exists primarily to look after the interests of its own nation, even though an enlightened self-interest, if nothing more, requires that it do something for others. But just as the purely voluntary principle of wage restraint by independent unions in Britain has not worked, I do not believe that voluntary contributions to finance U.N. military operations will prove feasible—though of course there can be no reason why any system which is adopted should bar additional voluntary contributions from countries or organizations. More than all this, however, I consider that the method adopted for actually paying the soldiers in the Congo was wrong. Put briefly, the system (as explained to me in the Congo) was to pay each contingent whatever rates the supplying country notified to the U.N. as being payable for the service of its forces overseas. Many of the countries concerned had never had contingents serving abroad; some of the countries had indeed only existed for a year or two; and some took full advantage of the invitation to make out their own bills. The Guinea battalion, for example, came to the Congo with a multi-star general (who had donned uniform for the first time in this operation). He had to be paid $80 a day as his overseas allowance, in addition to free lodging, a car and chauffeur, and so on. That kind of expenditure by the U.N. was wholly unjustified; and different rates of pay for troops living in the same place and doing the same work produced the same sort of ill-feeling as has been evident in many places elsewhere when similar situations obtained. What is the answer? I believe that the right thing would have been for the U.N. to supply (in kind and never in cash) the accommodation and food to which each unit was accustomed, or could reasonably in the circumstances be expected to put up with; and for the supplying country to pay its troops whatever cash at home or in local spending money it chose to grant. In the case of the richer nations, most of the pay could have been banked at home for use on return. All troops should have worn the same uniform. And for the kind of duties which the troops were being called upon to perform, there could have been no objection to a fairly rapid turnover, e.g. three months. This would have cost more in transport; but savings on pay would have been an offset. Some such system would be possible for the small tasks—such as the Gaza Strip or Cyprus.

But the nub of the U.N. peace-keeping operations is to keep the peace when fighting threatens; and for this an entirely different approach is needed. Maybe for long we shall still have to put up with the second-best; and in that case let us, of course, get that as good as we can. But we should be clear that there is a strict limit on what can be achieved in this way. If we hope that one day the U.N., in its present form or more likely with a different constitution, will indeed be a world authority, then it must—if that phrase is not to be a contradiction in terms —dispose of sufficient force to assert its authority. And that force must be its own force. The ultimate answer for U.N. peace-keeping forces must therefore be that the U.N. should recruit and build up a balanced force for itself. How quickly such a force can be created and how strong it should be is a matter for the political will of the countries of the world. The more the citizen is prepared to accept the authority of the police, the less well-armed the police need to be. We are a long way from that kind of international thinking at present; but if we do not want to make false steps in the meanwhile, we should try to be clear where it is that we are trying in the end to reach. There is no reason either why a beginning should not be made just as soon as sufficient agreement can be reached to start a U.N. force—both by life secondment and simul-taneously by recruitment for a lifetime of service. Before forces can be recruited, a headquarters organization will have to be set up; and a beginning could be made now with this.

The availability of an effective force is one aspect of the matter: another is the control and the definition of the political objectives which the U.N. is hoping to achieve. This touches the core of the U.N. Organization. By 1960 the U.N. had almost got to the point when the Organization as such could take important initiatives. That was in Hammarskjøld's time when his skill and subtlety in interpreting Resolutions seemed for a brief while to be developing for the U.N. a certain freedom and flexibility of action with, at times, considerable and almost general backing—or at least a refraining from opposition. But that phase passed and Hammarskjøld died; it seems unlikely that a similar favourable concatenation of circumstances can recur. This is no reflection on the present or any future holder of the office of Secretary-General. But what with the passage of time and the inclusion of many more members; the bitterness engendered over China, Vietnam, Rhodesia, and South Africa; the world's financial difficulties; and the spreading realization that the population problem, for which the U.N. can do little, is the major world problem for the rest of this century— all these, and more intangible changing attitudes, have removed perhaps for good even that slight possibility of organic development in the Organization as its Charter now is.

The inability to formulate and change (with changing needs) U.N. objectives has important consequences which the Congo strikingly exemplified. When Mobutu made his bloodless coup in the Congo in September 1960 and installed the Commissioners, there was no doubt at all that he succeeded to Lumumba's crumbling authority. But the U.N. Organization would not or could not recognize him in that capacity. In fact it was reluctantly compelled to do so *de facto*, but withheld *de jure* recognition.

The third and probably most important aspect of the U.N.'s handling of change is the problem of how to reach a settlement of disputes before they become acute. It is only in this latter case that the Security Council can be seized of a situation—when it has already become dangerous enough to be a threat to international peace. But something more is wanted than that; and something different from the International Court which can only decide on the legal aspects of a dispute. Another peace-keeping organ of the U.N. is needed—which can take account of political, perhaps economic and social also, aspects of a dispute between countries—which could for example deal with a problem such as the Sudetenland posed in the thirties; or the current dispute over Gibraltar, or boundary differences between South American states. It is necessary to recognize the problems before we can hope to find an answer and to arrange procedures and machinery to settle international disputes peacefully before the stage is reached of having to use force at all. So we need to strive after four objectives.

The first is the organization of the U.N. so that its peace-keeping role can be positive, flexible, and sensitive before a dispute becomes actual; perhaps the International Court can play a part in this, but much more than a legal approach is needed. The second is the setting up of a system for the control of a U.N. military force in the light of the political directive it is expected to carry out, so that the final result is universally acceptable afterwards if force has to be used. The third—how to provide the U.N. with a continuous stream of intelligence and information on which it can base its decisions: in my opinion this requires that the U.N. should have its own accredited representatives in all the capitals of the world. This would be a career civil service, akin to the military, of lifelong servants of the U.N. with loyalty to the Organization and not to their original countries. And the fourth is to make the necessary changes in the constitution of the U.N. itself to enable it to fulfil these various functions. It seems clear to me that it is unreal to expect Rwanda and Russia to have the same voice in the affairs of the world, and the U.N.'s constitution must be altered in a way which takes account of this fact of international life. If it is not, then we perpetuate a state of affairs which is unsatisfactory in practice because it is false in theory (that is not to say, of course, that an inhabitant of Rwanda should not have the same basic human rights as an inhabitant of Russia). If this is true, then a new look at the world organization in the light both of the needs it has to serve and the means it must dispose of in order to serve these ends is the essential next step. When the time comes for it to be taken, a greatly strengthened body will result.

This whole subject is going far beyond the purposes of this book, and is only discussed here because I believe that it is altogether too facile to talk of strengthening the peace-keeping powers of the U.N.— whether the purely military or otherwise—without examining carefully and much more deeply what exactly is meant and how exactly it can be achieved. To do otherwise, year after year, is only to encourage false hopes among the peoples of the world. It is obvious also that the kind of suggestions here discussed would not apply in the near future where major interests of the leading powers were concerned. It is just con-ceivable, however, that out of spreading nuclear dangers a new beginning may come. It would be best if the nations of the world agreed volun-tarily to limit proliferation of atomic weapons and gradually to reduce them where they already exist. But if this approach fails, maybe the United States and Russia will be driven to agree on this one thing—that they will police the world jointly to prevent the creation of any nuclear weapons by other countries and, if those now possessing them will not voluntarily do so, jointly destroy both their stocks and their manufacturing capacity. One might even hope, if increasing danger drove us to this pass, that these two countries would be authorized to take such action by the United Nations. In all this we should be careful to see that the best is not the enemy of the good, and be content to plan, for the next decade or two, a system of world security which will admittedly not be able to guarantee the security of all the countries of the world but which, with the help of the super-powers, will increasingly be able to guarantee peace to the other countries of the world.

Conclusion

There had to be a Congo somewhere, some time, in Africa. It was too good to be true that twenty or so new African countries should put on, in varying degrees of immaturity, the outward trappings of independent democratic sovereignty and take their place as equals in the world community without the act putting too great a strain on even one of them. The Belgians did a great deal for the Congo in the eighty years during which they ruled it; but they failed to do the one thing which mattered. They did not teach the Congolese the rudiments of self-government. They left no self-standing machine of administration behind them, only a complicated democratic constitution which might have been good for some countries of Western Europe but was certainly not tailored to the needs of the Congo. The foreshortening of the transition period to a very few months in 1960 was frighteningly irresponsible and very many Belgians reacted by taking fright.

Kasavubu had urged at the Round Table Conference in January 1960 the immediate formation of a Congolese government, precisely in order to give the Congolese some desperately needed experience; but this had been refused. The council of six leading Congolese politicians which was set up had only limited collective responsibility, along with the Governor-General who retained the power. In the last weeks before Independence, when effective power both at the centre and in the provinces was obviously and disastrously slipping from Belgian hands, a special Minister was sent out from Brussels to stiffen the administration. It was, however, a time for suppleness and for the greatest skill in trying to effect a smooth hand-over of power. Moreover, the basis of power in the Congo was tribal (except for the army) and the constitution which Belgium bequeathed to the Congo reflected a different conception—a strong unitary state with centralized power. This dichotomy between the real and pretended bases of power was a serious complication when the crisis came. In a way it was not so remarkable that confusion developed, as that the country did not completely disintegrate. This was a tribute to the momentum which the Belgians gave it even though law and order, economic life, public health, communications, education, and every other activity of government seriously deteriorated. It was not only the inexperience of the Congolese in the arts of government that prolonged their country's agony: they were grappling with constitutional and political problems which were inherently difficult and complicated and which would have taxed the capacity of much more mature leaders. It took, after all, several years and a number of conferences in London for a Nigerian constitution to be worked out. The Congo is much larger (though less populous) than Nigeria and as diverse, and had had a score of graduates at Independence as against thousands in Nigeria; and even there painful and lengthy adjustments are having to be made to meet the facts of tribalism and the tendencies to separatism.

The history of the year July 1960 to July 1961 was largely a history of the Congolese Army; sometimes violently in the foreground of events, as during July and August 1960, but always in the background as a force with which to reckon. Lumumba called for help from the United Nations when the army mutinied within days of the Independence of the country; and an enormous and costly effort was made by the U.N. in response. It was the military aspect which was both the most immediately important and the most spectacular, an admirable fire-brigade operation which played its part in curbing excesses in various places; although it was not nearly as effective in some places even in this role as it might have been. This qualification has to be made, and was due not only to the quality of some of the U.N. military contingents but to the fact that, politically, the U.N. saw itself in a role which led to unfortunate consequences. It maintained that it was the neutral outsider which tried to ensure some kind of fair play, but itself declined to take any part in the settlement of the political problem. In strict theory there was something to be said for this; but the impact of the U.N. was so dominant that willy-nilly the U.N. became a participant in the Congo's affairs. Under imaginative and sympathetic leadership it could have played a vital role in helping to reconcile differences—but always by offering its help with due respect for Congolese sensibilities. Instead, it allowed its practices to be adapted to comply with the pressures from those who were not interested in fair play for the Congo and in the finding of the right solution, but only in furthering personal or national ambitions. Mobutu's military coup put an end to Nkrumah's activities and the inrush of Russian and Czech technicians, as well as other attempts to influence the Congo's efforts to find its own solution for its problems. This search was protracted however by the inflexible belief of the U.N. in its brand of 'neutralism', which led, for example, U.N.

forces to free Gizenga from arrest in Léopoldville and speed him on his way to Stanleyville, thus opening up a chapter of misery and horror which lasted for many months. Even in Stanleyville, when Gizenga was unable to overthrow the provincial government which had been in power from the time of Independence, the U.N. forces gave him refuge and protection until he could get outside help to enable him to do so.

Finally, one should perhaps comment on the psychological change towards the U.N. which the evidence of its work produced. In July 1960 there were the most tremendous expectations of what would result from a U.N. presence. Within a very few weeks, the whole attitude of the Congolese towards the U.N. had altered because the U.N. Organization lacked the flexibility to adapt itself to changing circumstances in the Congo. It found itself wholly unable to reach an accommodation with a military coup d'état and could use neither the criteria of recognition of *de facto* power nor the sort of moral criteria by which sometimes a country seems to determine its recognition of new regimes. Circumscribed by its own U.N. constitution, irrespective of the fact that this enshrines concepts of a political way of life which is alien to perhaps a majority of its members, the U.N. was caught up in a legalistic approach to problems which were not legal. It must be said that it was because it suited some of the U.N.'s members (so long as their own countries were not at the bar) to use the forum of New York and stand forth as champions of liberty and parliamentary democracy, that the agony in the Congo was prolonged. The consequence of this speciously correct but fundamentally false attitude was that the presence of the U.N. in the Congo frustrated the capacity of the more moderate elements of the country to take over control of the whole country. Moreover, to carry out its mission in the Congo the U.N. selected as its chosen instruments persons who in both civil amd military fields belonged to countries which could be labelled in New York as neutral. The plain fact was—and was clearly demonstrated in the Congo— that such countries as Sweden, Ireland, the Sudan, and—for other reasons—even India, either did not contain or were not willing to produce the kind of people required to control the Congo operation. In both civil and military fields the magnitude and intricacy of the task would have taxed the capacities of the world's leading administrators and military commanders. Further, the United Nations was neither conceived nor organized to cope with a situation like the Congo; hence, those who were in charge of its operations on the spot failed to derive from the Organization either the intelligence assessments or the steady enlightened advice of which they had need. The staff of the United Nations in the Congo was in the main haphazardly recruited from U.N. Headquarters and from the associated and subsidiary organizations of the U.N. such as UNESCO, I.L.O., and so on. This produced the oddest results, as when a junior interpreter suddenly became a senior political adviser. Inevitably there was a lack of understanding all round. For a brief time in the spring of 1961 the U.N. functioned in the Congo as it ideally should have done all along; but that phase ended soon after Mekki Abbas left, to be succeeded by Linner. Things reverted to a degree which led a leading African member of the U.N. Organization to write, as he told me, to Bunche, 'It is both difficult and painful to work for white men in Africa.' From a devoted and able servant of the U.N., a liberal Ghanaian, such a remark was a tragic commentary on the continued inadequacy of the direction of the U.N., both in the Congo and in New York. And, just before I finally left the Congo, General Iyassou, the Ethiopian deputy supreme commander of the U.N. forces and a very fine officer and person, told me that he was glad to be leaving. He felt he said, that the U.N. could never handle the Congo aright until New York was prepared to put first the interests of the Congolese, and not the effects which each decision would have on the voting on some quite other matter in the Assembly.

Perhaps the true explanation of the U.N.'s inadequacy in that first year—despite all that it achieved—is that the various Security Council Resolutions embodied conflicting ideas, because of conflicting pressures in New York, of what the U.N. was to do in the Congo. No clear guidance could therefore be given from New York. Maybe this is something which is inherent in the nature of the U.N. as at present constituted, and which becomes evident when ambitions and emotions are aroused, preventing the dispassionate consideration of a problem. Certainly in its dealings with the Congo, the U.N. spent far too much time and effort in agreeing texts of Resolutions in New York, and too little in considering the relevance of these Resolutions to the problems in the Congo.

Appendix

Translation of letters from Lumumba, as subsequently published in the press, referred to on p. 81.

I

(for reproduction of original as published, see Plate 5)

REPUBLIC OF THE CONGO

Léopoldville,
15 September, 1960

OFFICE OF THE PRIME MINISTER

STRICTLY CONFIDENTIAL

SUBJECT:
Measures to be applied in the first phase of dictatorship

To M. FINANT
President of the Provincial
Government at Stanleyville

1 Annex

Dear Sir,

I enclose herewith your copy of the circular letter which I have sent today, on the subject named above.

For reasons of secrecy, I am delaying despatch of the copies for your Colleagues. I shall send them as soon as possible.

As all Orientale Province is in OUR HANDS, you will be able at once to take steps for the meticulous carrying out of these orders.

I promise you all my support if certain persons should attempt to intervene and criticize you in any way whatever.

Do not forget to give constant encouragement to our comrades throughout the Province, in assuring them that in conformity with the agreement, the CONGO will become what they have demanded of us.

Lastly, in your programme for the arrest of the members of the opposition and others, it will be convenient to begin with the most influential; such for example as: KUPA François, LOPES Antoine, EDINDALI André, TABALO, J., MOTTA . . ., all the leading chiefs and even some of your colleagues (members of the provincial Government) who will try to criticize you.

In acting in this way, everyone in Stanleyville will fear Your Authority as they do mine here at Léopoldville. Thus, we shall end by leading all the inhabitants of the Republic by the nose like sheep, beginning with Orientale Province which is already in the power of our comrades in the East who, under the term 'technicians', have begun to cast, secretly and surely, the first lures of our doctrine.

Start the task at once and take courage.

LONG   LIVE   THE   SOVIET   UNION.   LONG   LIVE KHRUSCHEV.

The Prime Minister
[Signed] P. Lumumba.

N.B. This letter confirms my earlier verbal orders. Do not forget that it is because of the serious threats which I am continually uttering that the political balance lies in our favour.

II

REPUBLIC OF THE CONGO   *Léopoldville*
OFFICE OF THE PRIME MINISTER   15 September, 1960

STRICTLY CONFIDENTIAL
SUBJECT:
Measures to be applied in the first phase of dictatorship
To the President of the Provincial
Government (ALL) except Katanga.

Dear President,

I have the honour and the pleasure to bring to your knowledge that with a view to the early re-establishment of order in this country, the Chamber of Representatives and the Senate, meeting in extraordinary session on 13 September, have decided to invest the Government with full powers.

By FULL POWERS it must in fact be understood that the Government is free to act in everything and for every purpose as seems right to it, in order to suppress abuses, disorders, and all acts contrary to the will of the Government over which I have presided legally since the Congo became independent.

It is therefore necessary for the nationalist members of the Government, both centrally and provincially, to take advantage of this unique chance to bring about a state of order in the country and respect for established authority.

The most effective and direct means for the rapid success of our task can be summed up as follows:

(1) apply dictatorship thoroughly and in all its forms.

(2) terrorism, which is indispensable to dominate the people.

(3) proceed systematically and by means of the army, to arrest ALL THE MEMBERS OF THE OPPOSITION. I shall myself be responsible for those in Léopoldville, including the Head of State and his immediate supporters.

In view of the present situation in Katanga and South Kasai, I have sent, a few weeks ago, the National Army in order to arrest TSHOMBE and KALONJI and even to kill them if such a possibility offered. (In getting rid of these two persons as well as Mr. K. . ., the problems which beset us will be resolved without any difficulty.)

(4) imprison the Ministers, deputies, and senators who sometimes abuse their parliamentary immunity. If things reach such a pass, I shall be willing for you not to spare them and to arrest them all without mercy, reserving for them a treatment ten times more severe than what is proposed for ordinary individuals.

(5) bring back the DISCIPLINE OF THE WHIP and give ten strokes to the rebels, morning and evening, for seven successive days.

N.B. Double this treatment if it is a question of Ministers, senators, and deputies; thereafter, diminish the treatment progressively depending upon the state of each individual.

(6) make each of the people thus arrested suffer profound humiliation, apart from the mandatory treatment prescribed above. *For example*, strip them publicly and if possible in the presence of their wives and children. Make them carry a heavy burden and go on foot in this condition. In every case of such a walk they may be allowed to wear trousers.

(7) in view of the gravity of the situation which carries the risk of the country falling into anarchy, there is advantage in shutting up the recidivists in a cell or an underground prison for six months as a minimum, without ever giving them the chance to breathe clean air outside.

N.B. If it should happen that some die as a result of atrocities, which is both possible and desirable, steps should be taken not to give out the correct news, but to conceal the truth by announcing that Mr X has escaped and remains untraceable.

(8) those who do not die in prison will only be released after at least a year. In such a case, they will be exiled to a country which I shall decide upon myself in discussion with certain foreign countries which have already indicated to me their agreement in principle.

Some provincial Presidents will say to me that these measures are severe. I would reply at once that some politicians have arrived at power themselves by the use of dictatorial methods. The measures which I now direct are only the first phase of the regime which we hope to install in the Congo. The second will consist in bringing down everyone who criticizes us. . . .

To avoid ill-treating people of our own beliefs, in cases where they will not be known to you, it is necessary to send me at once the complete list and description of all people whom you have been led to arrest, in order to allow me to instruct you on the appropriate treatment for each individual.

By scrupulously carrying out these instructions which must come into force as soon as you receive this letter, I am convinced that we shall triumph.

Finally, I draw your attention to the fact that the authorities under your orders should not receive information about this present letter unless they enjoy your full confidence.

The Prime Minister
[Signed] P. Lumumba

Index